WRITERS AND THEIR WORK

ISOBEL ARMSTRONG
*General Editor*

BRYAN LOUGHREY
*Advisory Editor*



# GEORGE ELIOT

George Eliot

*from a chalk drawing of 1865 by* F. W. Burton *in the collection of the National Portrait Gallery, London*

# GEORGE ELIOT

**Josephine McDonagh**

NORTHCOTE

BRITISH COUNCIL

ATLANTIC
PUBLISHERS & DISTRIBUTORS (P) LTD

This edition is published by

**ATLANTIC**

PUBLISHERS & DISTRIBUTORS (P) LTD

7/22, Ansari Road, Darya Ganj, New Delhi-110 002
Tel: 40775252, 23273880, 23275880, 23280451; Fax: +91-11-23285873
E-mail: orders@atlanticbooks.com; Web: www.atlanticbooks.com

By arrangement with
**Northcote House Publishers Ltd**
Horndon House, Horndon, Tavistock, Devon, PL19 9NQ,
United Kingdom. (T)+44(0)1822 810066; (F)+44(0)1822 810034
(E) northcote.house@virgin.net and (W) www.northcotehouse.co.uk
The *Writers and their Work* series is published in association with
the British Council.


**First Indian Reprint 2010**
First published in 1997 by Northcote House Publishers Ltd

ISBN 978-81-269-1286-5



**British Library Cataloguing-in-Publication Data**
A catalogue record for this book is available from the British Library

Typeset by PDQ Typesetting, Newcastle-under-Lyme
Printed in India at Nice Printing Press, A-33/3A, Site-IV,
Industrial Area, Sahibabad, Ghaziabad, U.P.

For my aunt, Mary McDonagh

# Contents

# Acknowledgements

My thanks to Isobel Armstrong, and to Joe Bristow, Anne Janowitz, Colin Jones, Sally Ledger, Laura Marcus, and Robert Young.

# Biographical Outline

1819 22 November, born Mary Anne Evans, at South Farm, Arbury, Warwickshire, the third child of Robert Evans and Christiana Pearson. Evans also had two children by his previous wife.

1820 The Evans family move to Griff House, Chilvers Coton.

1824 Educated at Miss Latham's boarding school at Attleborough.

1828 Mrs Wallington's school at Nuneaton.

1832 Miss Franklin's School, Coventry.

1836 3 February, mother dies. Mary Anne leaves school.

1837 Chrissy Evans, Mary Anne's sister, marries, and Mary Anne is housekeeper to her father.

1841 Moves with father to Coventry. Her brother, Isaac, marries, and lives at Griff. Meets Charles and Cara Bray. Reads Charles Hennell's *An Inquiry into the Origins of Christianity*, a critical examination of the Gospels that demonstrates that Christianity is not a revealed religion, and fires Mary Anne's religious scepticism.

1842 Refuses to go to church in January, to Robert Evans's disapprobation. Reconciled when she resumes church attendance in May.

1844 Begins to translate D. F. Strauss, *Das Leben Jesu* (*The Life of Jesus, Critically Examined* (1846) ). Has a phrenological cast of her head made. Mesmerized at a party. Meets Harriet Martineau for the first time.

1849 31 May, father dies. Travels with the Brays to France, Italy, and Switzerland. Stays in Geneva for the winter with the painter François D'Albert Durade, and his wife.

1850 Returns to England. Reviews Mackay, *Progress of the Intellect*, for the *Westminster Review* (Jan. 1851).

1851 Moves to London and lodges with John Chapman and family in the Strand. Continues to write. In March she is thrown out of the house by Chapman's wife and mistress, but returns in September to becomes assistant editor to Chapman, who has recently acquired the *Westminster Review*. Meets George Combe, the phrenologist, and George Henry Lewes for the first time.

1852 Friendship with Herbert Spencer. Meets and befriends Barbara Leigh Smith (Bodichon).

1853 Deepening friendship with Lewes. Leaves Chapman's residence to take up separate lodgings in 21 Cambridge Street.

1854 Translation of Feuerbach, *Das Wesen des Christenthums* (*The Essence of Christianity*), published. 20 July, 'elopes' with Lewes to Germany. Writes articles for the *Westminster Review*, and begins translation of Spinoza, *Ethics*, while Lewes completes research for *Life of Goethe* (1855).

1855 Returns to England, lives in temporary lodgings with Lewes in London and East Sheen, until the couple set up house together in Richmond, Surrey.

1856 Articles for the *Westminster Review* include 'The Natural History of German Life' and 'Silly Novels by Lady Novelists'. Visits Ilfracombe and Tenby with Lewes, who is researching for *Sea-side Studies*. Begins to write fiction. 'The Sad Fortunes of Amos Barton' accepted by *Blackwood's Edinburgh Magazine* (1857).

1857 'Mr Gillfill's Love Story' and 'Janet's Repentance' published by *Blackwood's Edinburgh Magazine*. Adopts the pseudonym 'George Eliot' for the first time. Breaks with brother, Isaac, on revelation of her relationship with Lewes.

1858 'The Sad Fortunes of Amos Barton', 'Mr Gillfill's Love Story', and 'Janet's Repentance' published together as *Scenes of Clerical Life*. Letters of praise arrive from, among others, Dickens and Jane Carlyle. Travels to Germany and Austria.

1859 Moves to Holly Lodge, Wandsworth. *Adam Bede* published in three volumes to massive acclaim. George Eliot's identity revealed. Sister Chrissy dies. 'The Lifted Veil' published in *Blackwood's Edinburgh Magazine*. Travels to Switzerland.

1860 *The Mill on the Floss* published in three volumes. March–June, travels to Rome, Naples, Florence, and Switzerland. Moves to two further London addresses. Writes 'Brother Jacob'.

1861 *Silas Marner* published. Returns to Florence.

1862 *Romola* serialized in *Cornhill* (published in three volumes in 1863).

1863 Moves to The Priory, North Bank, Regent's Park.

1864 Travels again to Italy. Begins *The Spanish Gypsy*.

1865 Travels to Paris, and later, Brittany.

1866 *Felix Holt: The Radical* published in three volumes. Travels to Germany and the Low Countries. Friendship with Browning. Meets Lehmann.

1867 Lewes begins work on *Problems of Life and Mind* (5 vols., 1874–9). Donates £50 to the foundation of Girton College. Travels to the South of France, Spain, and returns through Germany.

1868 *The Spanish Gypsy* published. Travels to Germany and Switzerland.

1869 Begins correspondence with Harriet Beecher Stowe and friendship with the Burne-Joneses. Lewes's son, Thornton Lewes, returns from Natal. 19 October, Thornton dies. Travels to Italy. Meets John Cross and his mother in Rome.

1870 Travels to Germany, Prague, Austria.

1871 Summer spent at country house, Shottermill. Meets the Tennysons. 'Armgart' published. 1st book of *Middlemarch* published.

1872 Books 2–8 of *Middlemarch* published. Travels to Germany for a holiday. Meets Edith Simcox.

1873 Returns to Germany to visit the synagogues.

1874 *The Legend of Jubal and Other Poems*. Falls ill with a kidney stone from which she suffers intermittently until she dies.

1876 *Daniel Deronda* published in eight books. Buys The Heights, Witley, Surrey.

1877 Travels to France and Switzerland. Socializes with the Wagners. Dines with Princess Louise.

1878 Meets Turgenev. Lewes ill with cancer. 30 November, Lewes dies.

1879 Works on Lewes's *Problems of Life and Mind. The Impressions of Theophrastus Such* published.

1880 6 May, marries John Cross. Honeymoon on Continent. Return after Cross falls from balcony into the Grand Canal in Venice. 3 December, moves to Cross's house in Cheyne Walk. 19 December, falls ill with sore throat, which turns into a fever. 22 December, Eliot dies.

# Abbreviations

| | |
|---|---|
| *AB* | *Adam Bede*, ed. and intro. by Stephen Gill (Harmondsworth: Penguin, 1980) |
| *DD* | *Daniel Deronda*, ed. and intro. by Barbara Hardy (Harmondsworth: Penguin, 1967) |
| *E.* | *Selected Essays, Poems and Other Writings*, ed. A. S. Byatt and Nicholas Warren (Harmondsworth: Penguin, 1990) |
| *EC* | Ludwig A. Feuerbach, *The Essence of Christianity* (*Das Wesen des Christenthums*), trans. from the 2nd edn. by Marian Evans (London: John Chapman, 1854) |
| *FH* | *Felix Holt: The Radical*, ed. and intro. by Lynda Mugglestone (Harmondsworth: Penguin, 1995) |
| *GEB* | Gordon S. Haight, *George Eliot: A Biography* (1968; Harmondsworth: Penguin, 1992) |
| *L.* | *The George Eliot Letters*, ed. Gordon S. Haight, 9 vols. (New Haven, Conn.: Yale University Press, 1954–5, 1978) |
| *M.* | *Middlemarch*, ed. and intro. by Rosemary Ashton (Harmondsworth: Penguin, 1994) |
| *MF* | *The Mill on the Floss*, ed. and intro. by A. S. Byatt (Harmondsworth: Penguin, 1979) |
| *R.* | *Romola*, ed. and intro. by Andrew Sanders (Harmondsworth: Penguin, 1980) |
| *SC* | *Scenes of Clerical Life*, ed. and intro. by David Lodge (Harmondsworth: Penguin, 1973) |
| *SM* | *Silas Marner*, ed. and intro. by Q. D. Leavis (Harmondsworth: Penguin, 1967) |
| *TS* | *The Impressions of Theophrastus Such*, ed. D. J. Enright (London: Everyman, 1995) |

# Prologue: Approaching Eliot

> I can see her descending the great staircase of our house in Savile Row...on my father's arm, the only lady, except my mother, among the group of remarkable men, politicians, and authors of the first literary rank. She would talk and laugh softly, and look up into my father's face respectfully, while the light of the great hall-lamp shone on the waving masses of her hair, and the black velvet [dress] fell in folds about her feet
>
> Bessie R. Belloc [Parkes][1]

George Eliot's death from a sore throat caught at a performance of *Agamemnon* brought to an end one of the glittering literary careers of the century. She had become a renowned international celebrity, fêted by royalty, and esteemed by intellectuals and artists from across the world. Turgenev had deemed her 'the greatest living novelist', and Henry James wrote that he had 'fall[en] in love with her' when they met in 1869. After the publication of her novels, appreciative readers had sent gifts of books, flowers, even game.[2] In an essay published in 1885, the historian Lord Acton recorded her position in the public estimation as 'the greatest genius among women known to history'.[3]

Eliot's career as a novelist, on which this fame was based, had begun only twenty-four years before then, when she was thirty-seven. Indeed it was then that 'George Eliot', the pseudonym invented for the publication of her fiction, came into existence. In 1857 *Blackwood's Magazine* published her first substantial work of fiction, 'The Sad Fortunes of Amos Barton', one of the three stories that make up *Scenes of Clerical Life* (1858). Seven weighty novels followed: *Adam Bede* (1859), *The Mill on the Floss* (1860),

*Silas Marner* (1861), *Romola* (1863), *Felix Holt: The Radical* (1866), *Middlemarch* (1871–2), and *Daniel Deronda* (1876). But although her reputation was made as a novelist, she was in fact a more wide-ranging writer than this. Her *œuvre* contains other kinds of work: novellas ('The Lifted Veil' (1859) and 'Brother Jacob' (1864) ), a series of essays entitled *The Impressions of Theophrastus Such* (1879), and poetry (*The Spanish Gypsy* (1861), 'Armgart' (1871), and *The Legend of Jubal and Other Poems* (1874) ). Even before she became 'George Eliot', as Mary Ann Evans (her birth name), or Marian Evans (as she later called herself),[4] she had translated major works of philosophy and theology from the German (D. F. Strauss, *The Life of Jesus, Critically Examined* (1846), Ludwig Feuerbach, *The Essence of Christianity* (1854), and Spinoza, *Ethics* (begun, 1854, first published in 1981) ), and had written numerous essays and reviews mostly for the *Westminster Review.* From 1851 to 1854 she was the assistant editor of the *Westminster Review,* the leading liberal publication of the day, a role that in fact accorded her full editorial responsibility. By anyone's standards, these were brilliant literary and intellectual achievements.

However, Eliot gained not only literary acclaim; she also accrued considerable moral prestige. As Bernard Semmel notes in *George Eliot and the Politics of National Inheritance* (1994), in her own lifetime Eliot came to occupy the revered position of a moral guide within a period of changing religious and social views. He cites the historian G. M. Young's claim in 1936 that she had 'saved us from the moral catastrophe which might have been expected to follow upon the waning of religious conviction'.[5] The idea that Eliot's work is morally redemptive, capable of supplying secure moral values in a profane world, is a theme that comes to the fore in much of the criticism of her work. F. R. Leavis, writing in 1948, elected Eliot to the quartet of outstanding English novelists, whose works embody what he called *The Great Tradition,* a repository of fine moral judgements and humane values that he considered to be characteristically English.[6] Even as recently as 1993, Alan Bellringer, echoing Leavis, mused that, had she lived, Eliot would have saved the country from 'the decadence, jingoism and socialist uplift which swept British culture in the *fin de siècle*.'[7] To be ascribed this position of moral and cultural saviour – much like one of her characters – is a significant achievement. But it is all the more remarkable for a woman who had transgressed one of the most important social conventions of the time: for over twenty years, Eliot lived openly with another woman's husband. As a consequence, she spent most of her adult life as something of an embarrassment in polite company, relegated to the peripheries of respectable society.

She met her life partner, George Henry Lewes, for the first time in 1851, in a book shop in the Burlington Arcade. By then, his marriage to Agnes Jervis (by whom he had four children) had already broken down irreparably. Lewes (1817–78) was an experienced and extraordinarily versatile writer himself. G. S. Haight notes in his biography of Eliot that by 1850 Lewes had already published 'a popular history of philosophy, two novels, a life of Robespierre, a tragedy in blank verse produced at Manchester, Liverpool and London, besides scores of successful periodical articles of a wide variety of subjects' (*GEB* 127). His most important literary work was his two-volume biography of Goethe (1855), but later it was science, in particular biology, that came to preoccupy him. His works in this area include *Sea-side Studies* (1858), *The Physiology of Common Life* (1859), and his multi-volumed pioneering study of psychology, *Problems of Life and Mind* (1873–9). Agnes had had a long-standing affair with Lewes's friend and collaborator, Thornton Leigh Hunt, and, in 1850 and 1851, bore two children by him. Perhaps admitting a role in the deterioration of their relationship, Lewes accepted these children as his own, but under the laws of the day, this acknowledgement of another man's children meant that he had condoned his wife's adultery, and thus was unable to obtain a divorce. As the love affair between Lewes and Marian Evans intensified, they came to the decision that, even though they would never be free to marry, they should live together as man and wife.[8] In July 1854 they left for Germany – at the time Lewes was researching for his biography of Goethe – after which they returned to England, and lived together happily until Lewes's death in 1878. From their 'elopement' onwards, Marian called herself 'Mrs Lewes'.

Those who knew the couple realized that their relationship was an ideal one, bringing emotional and intellectual fulfilment to both;[9] but in the eyes of the law and society, it could never be more than a shady and illicit union. It cost Marian her relations with her family – she was cut off by her revered elder brother, Isaac – and social respectability. Even after the success of her novels, she was shunned by respectable middle-class society, in particular married women, and, as a consequence, she and Lewes led a somewhat reclusive personal life – but one that was suited to the intense intellectual life they shared. Indeed, the pseudonym 'George Eliot' was a ruse to veil her true identify not as a woman, as is often presumed, but specifically as a *fallen* woman, as she was then considered to be. She and Lewes were only too aware of the moral stain that her domestic situation, if it were known, would leave on her published work. Her true identity – leaked by gossiping friends[10] – emerged after the publication of her first full-length novel, *Adam Bede*, in 1859, and its immediate effect was her public denunciation. One prominent magazine, the *Athenaeum*, deemed her a 'strong-minded lady, blessed with abundance of showy sentiment and a profusion of pious words, but kept for sale rather than for use', and the work was dismissed as being of 'no great quality'.[11] But, as damaging as such words were, *Scenes of Clerical Life* and *Adam Bede* had already achieved such popularity that her literary reputation withstood this attack. Indeed, Eliot presents the interesting example of a woman writer who challenges the stereotypes with which we tend to associate Victorian morality: while her 'immoral' domestic arrangements were generally known, and rumours about her supposed sexual voraciousness circulated widely, nevertheless her works were considered to be arbiters of moral and cultural value. Notions of respectability were, even then, much more complex and flexible (and contradictory) than we might expect.

Eliot did in fact marry in the last year of her life, but not to Lewes, who had died of cancer eighteen months earlier. On 6 May 1880, in St George's Church, Hanover Square, London, she sealed a union with John Cross, twenty years her junior, and a close family friend whom she and Lewes used to call 'Nephew'. At the wedding, she was 'given away' by Lewes's son, Charles Lewes. Johnny Cross was a stockbroker who had given the couple financial advice in their later years, and, after Lewes's death, had provided much needed practical help to Eliot. The marriage was short-lived – Eliot died just six months later; but after her death Cross devoted his energies to preparing a biography of Eliot, *George Eliot's Life*, which was published in three volumes in 1885.

Cross's biography of his wife is an unusual work in that it endeavours to present the life in the subject's own words: passages from her correspondence and journals are knitted together into a continuous narrative with relatively little direct editorial comment. Nevertheless, the words are heavily edited, and the life that emerges is very much moulded by Cross, the devoted widower. Despite the quirks of Eliot's unorthodox sexual past, Cross portrays a woman who very much accords with Victorian standards of womanhood. For instance, he notes her desire to be 'above all things, feminine', and that she was a proud and enthusiastic home-maker.[12] He carefully selected the passages of her correspondence to include in the work, and even destroyed some of her own journal from the 1849–54 period, presumably to protect her reputation. Moreover, he failed to consult some of Eliot's more radical friends – for instance, the socialist activist, Edith Simcox, who had fallen passionately in love with Eliot, and whose journal has provided later biographers with valuable insights into Eliot's life.[13] Throughout Cross stresses Eliot's heightened capacity for feeling rather than for thought, and her remarkable sensitivity manifest in her physical delicacy (both she and Lewes were plagued with ill health), which for him was the basis of her faculty for fine moral judgements. Significant too is the emphasis that he lays on her girlhood at Griff, the farmhouse in which she grew up in the countryside near Coventry, and the rural influence which, according to Cross, best explains her subsequent literary works. On the other hand, he downplays the significance on her writing of her experience as the editor of one of the country's leading journals, her continental travels with Lewes, her life among the most prominent scientists and thinkers of her day. The Eliot that emerges from Cross is very much the respectable daughter of provincial England, not the urban intellectual and cosmopolitan writer who lived for most of her adult life with the mercurial Lewes – a man who preferred even casual conversation in French.[14]

Although Cross's version of Eliot was very much a product of his own fashioning, it complemented and endorsed many of the assessments of her literary works in the period directly following her death, and continuing well into the next century. She was most ardently admired as the novelist of provincial England. Her works were considered a repository of middle-class social memory, depicting an England that was largely lost through the incursions of industrialization. Descriptions of places such as Hayslope in *Adam Bede*, or St Oggs in *The Mill on the Floss*, had implanted in the public imagination the memory of a way of life and a place that together encapsulated the essential components of Englishness: a rural environment, and a set of traditional social relationships, which are hierarchical, but characterized by a spirit of beneficence and community. Moreover, such descriptions were appreciated because they seemed so substantial and realistic; many readers felt that her novels presented true documentary evidence of a lived historical past. Cross's biography thus set the terms for a pervasive critical tradition that saw Eliot as a specifically English writer, a novelist of feeling rather than of ideas, and the guardian of the memory of a past way of life and traditional moral values.

It is easy to see how her reputation as a champion of a realistic yet nostalgic view of a disappearing England might take shape. Most of her works are set in provincial England. Only *Romola*, in Renaissance Florence, and her long poem, *The Spanish Gypsy*, are situated wholly outside England. In *Daniel Deronda* characters roam freely from England to the Continent, and, at the end of the novel, Daniel, his new wife, Mirah, and her brother, Mordecai, set off for Jerusalem to establish a Jewish homeland; but this novel, as I shall argue in Chapter 3, is radically different from the others in its apprehension of the relationships between people and places. Apart from Dorothea's and Casaubon's brief sojourn to Rome in *Middlemarch*, the action of the other novels is solidly situated in England. Moreover, Eliot always locates her novels in the past – usually between forty and sixty years previous to the date of writing: for instance, *Adam Bede* is set at the turn of the nineteenth century, and the events of *Felix Holt* and *Middlemarch* take place in the early 1830s. But to regard Eliot as a nostalgic writer, or an uncritical traditionalist, underestimates the extent to which her work, rather than exalting or even mourning the past, examines the processes of social and cultural change within a community or a nation in a much more positive and analytical way. As we shall see, the central questions to which all her works return are to do with social and cultural change: what are the mechanisms for change? how is change generated? and how is it incorporated into people's lives? Thus, although her works are set in the past, this is never a monolithic, unchanging past.

If we look more carefully at the period settings of Eliot's novels, we will notice that she has chosen historical moments not because they are static and stable, but, on the contrary, because they are pivotal ones: moments at which changes in the organization of commerce, or the law, or developments in science and technology take place, or at which the political structure of the entire nation is on the brink of change, such as the time of the first Reform Bill that provides the backdrop to *Felix Holt* and *Middlemarch*. The decisive event lying behind the intricacies of the plot in *The Mill on the Floss* is a change in irrigation technology, adversely affecting the livelihood of the Tullivers, which is presented as a metonym for the technological developments of the Industrial Revolution. *Romola* is set at the end of the Italian Renaissance, whose role as a foundational moment in Western culture had recently been expounded by Jakob Burckhardt in his *The Civilization of the Italian Renaissance* (1860), and the events of *Daniel Deronda* take place amid the nationalist struggles of the mid-1860s – the formation of new nation states in Europe (Germany, Italy), and the American Civil War.

Eliot's novels tell stories not of static and unchanging societies, but of societies in the midst of change. In particular she focuses on processes of uneven development, in which advances in science and technology, for instance, or in individual development brought about through education, cannot immediately be incorporated within existing society. For example, in *Middlemarch*, the physician Lydgate's zeal for medical reform is thwarted by the resistance of the community to the social changes that his new scientific ideas would necessitate; or, in *The Mill on the Floss*, the development of the heroine Maggie Tulliver's humanitarian consciousness puts her out of step with the conservative and repressive society of St Oggs. The belief that informs all her novels is that the development of knowledge – in particular, of scientific knowledge – is possible only under the right social conditions; and, conversely, that developments in knowledge will always have a corresponding effect on the fabric of society. In most cases, this effect will be a positive one, for Eliot holds to the broadly progressive view that knowledge generally works in the interest of social improvement. But nevertheless new ideas should be introduced gently and in ways which respect the organic fabric of society, imposed not abruptly or violently from above or outside, but with the consent of the existing society. She believes in improvement and adaptation, not revolution, whether political (as in *Felix Holt* and *Middlemarch*) or cultural (*Romola*). In *Middlemarch*, for instance, Caleb Garth, the improving estate manager, is presented as the acceptable face of modernization, rather than Lydgate or Ladislaw, the radical. (According to the biographers, Garth is the man in the mould of Eliot's father, Robert Evans, who was also a farmer and manager of estates.) While Lydgate runs roughshod over the existing medical mores of Middlemarch, Garth tempers his desire to implement the best new agricultural techniques with a sensitivity to traditional knowledge and farming practices, embodying all the values that Eliot credits most highly: an interest in experimentation and scientific progress *combined with* an attendance to custom, but above ail, a sympathetic appreciation of the needs of others.

Thus the characterization of Eliot that was encouraged by Cross's biography as a traditionalist, or a conservative, a nostalgic preserver of the values of provincial England, underplays her measured support for social progress; she believed that scientific discovery and technological knowledge could and should work in the interests of social improvement. While this does not make her in any sense a politically radical writer, it does make her a different kind of writer from the one portrayed by Cross, and one who engages with questions or tradition and modernity in a much more complex and challenging way than criticism within the moral tradition has sometimes allowed.

In fact, it was another biography of Eliot that laid the foundations for the more recent critics to reconsider the works in the context of the intellectual, cultural, and political questions of her day. G. S. Haight's *George Eliot: A Biography* (1968), which until recently remained the most authoritative account of Eliot's life,[15] highlights the dynamic intellectual culture in which Eliot was a significant player. Like Cross, Haight draws heavily on

Eliot's correspondence and journals, but his concern is less with painting a portrait of a respectable Victorian lady than with depicting her development as a substantial intellectual and literary figure who was part of a network of prominent scientists, philosophers, artists, and writers. Among her immediate circle were figures such as the evolutionary scientist and sociologist Herbert Spencer, the feminist reformer Barbara Bodichon, the artist Edward Burne-Jones, and the poet laureate Alfred Tennyson. Throughout her life, she also knew, met, or corresponded as an equal with some of the most significant figures of the era: for instance, the inventor Charles Babbage, scientists Charles Darwin and T. H. Huxley, the painter Frederic Lehmann, poets Robert Browning and Ralph Waldo Emerson, composers Franz Liszt and Richard Wagner, and writers Thomas Carlyle, Harriet Martineau, Harriet Beecher Stowe, and William Makepeace Thackeray. Indeed, Haight's biography of Eliot presents a rich and informative picture of Victorian metropolitan cultural life. Within this context, Eliot cuts an interesting figure whose personal life was directly shaped by her intellectual life: not only her ideas and beliefs, but also, more generally, her intellectual interests directly determined the social environment she inhabited and, indeed, her vocation. This is particularly evident in the decade that preceded her move to London in 1851, when, through her social network in Coventry, she met, and subsequently became friends with, Cara and Charles Bray, and Cara's sister, Sara Hennell. The Brays were free thinkers and their influence led to Eliot's renunciation, at the age of 22, of her hitherto profound Evangelical beliefs. Through Bray and his circle she became familiar with various radical and challenging ideas, many of them coming from the Continent, and which Eliot herself, as a translator, would be instrumental in introducing into British culture: in particular works of German philosophy, such as D. F. Strauss's influential survey of the life of Christ, *Das Leben Jesu,* crucial in the development of a school of historical biblical criticism known as Higher Criticism, which examined religious texts as historical documents rather than works that revealed religious truth. Through Bray, himself an enthusiastic follower of phrenology and friend of the influential phrenologist, George Combe, she also became interested in the fringe sciences that had a surprisingly wide impact during this period, and which we shall discuss in Chapter 3. And through Bray, too, she met John Chapman, who became the owner and editor of the *Westminster Review*, and with whom Eliot lodged and worked in London after the death of her father and before her union with Lewes, so beginning a new episode in her life.

The acknowledgement of her place within this broader culture was one of the positive contributions of Haight's biography to Eliot scholarship. It has had a profound impact on recent critical assessments of Eliot, enabling a treatment of the themes in her works in terms of *ideas* rather than in terms of feeling. For example, the social relations depicted in Eliot's works have been usefully examined in terms of nineteenth-century philosophical beliefs about community, and the developing discipline of sociology;[16] her significant friendships with women, including leading feminist reformers and activists such as Barbara Bodichon, Bessie Raynor Parkes, and Edith Simcox, have provided the basis for examining Eliot's treatment of the various political and social issues which, in this period, came under the heading of the 'Woman Question';[17] and her relations with Lewes and Spencer have led some critics to uncover in her works a profound engagement with scientific questions of contemporary concern, evidenced not only in themes and references within the texts, but also in the very structure of their narratives.[18] Examined as works that engage seriously with a broad range of questions of contemporary concern, her writings emerge as significant and complex cultural documents – more than the record of a sensitive individual's feelings, or statements of enduring moral truths, as they had previously been regarded. Although Eliot's life provides the impetus for this work, it tends to be less concerned with her personality than with broader social or cultural issues that are raised by and in her works.

A particular feature of these cultural and history-of-ideas approaches to Eliot's work has been to offer insight into the way in which her works provide a forum for the discussion of a surprisingly wide range of non-literary debates, from arenas such as science, politics, or philosophy. In her range of interests, Eliot is no less broad than Lewes, a writer who ranged across a remarkable variety of fields. But, while Lewes purposefully shifted genres to address a specialist audience in each field he took up – for example, in history, biology, or psychology – Eliot adapted the very flexible form of the novel in order to incorporate discussion of the pressing intellectual issues of the day. Ironically, as a writer of fiction, she managed to reach a far larger audience than Lewes or other specialist writers of the time were able to – but an audience which was perhaps unaware of the intellectual and philosophical context from which Eliot emerged. The thrust of recent approaches to Eliot has been to restore her works to this context. Rather than reading them as uncomplicated documents of an enduring reality, critics have begun to see them as complex texts that weave together various kinds of ideas about the world that had a special pertinence in the intellectual debates of the period – ideas to do with evolution, the organization of society, the place and responsibilities of the individual, or the limits of social progress.

The present study draws on the methods and findings of recent Eliot scholarship. The writer we shall explore in these pages is not the writer-genius, oracle of universal and unchanging moral truths, but the Victorian intellectual, solidly rooted in the conditions and culture of her own time. She was a writer who not only wrote about the central questions of her time, but one who had been formed, and whose literary ambitions had been formed, in the very society about which she wrote. Part of the concern, therefore, is to provide a cultural map in which to situate her works: in particular we will examine the ways in which she takes up contemporary debates in various branches of science and medicine, and in sociology, or social theory. A complex network of interests and relations will emerge, providing the structure or frame around which she weaves her narratives.

It is important to be aware of this frame, for it provides the basis for a corrective against a tendency among readers to mistake her novels as unmediated accounts of 'real life'. For many, her most compelling feature is her ability to describe situations and events as though they had in fact occurred within the real world. The problem with such an approach is that it accepts too easily her version of the world as the accurate and acceptable one. It misses the polemical edge to her work – the fact that, rather than documenting reality, her fiction spins arguments about its components: issues such as, for instance, the proper organization of society, or the effects of technological change, or the impact of new forms of scientific understanding. The fact that readers are willing to believe so easily in the truth of Eliot's fiction is testament to the success of her techniques as a realist writer. But, by the same count, it also suggests that we must examine these techniques to understand the ways in which they operate.

The discussion that follows is organized into three thematically based chapters, each of which takes up a different aspect of realism in her work. The first chapter explores her use of description – the obsessive documentation of details of material life – which is the hallmark of her realism. The second analyses a motif that occurs in all her works and which is crucial to her representation of social reality – the idea of the family. For Eliot this provides not only an index of social reality, but also a model of social relations and, as a generative unit, a model for social change. In this second chapter, then, I consider the uses of the family in Eliot's configurations of historical change. Finally I will examine the works that for various reasons do not fit into the realist model: 'The Lifted Veil', *Daniel Deronda,* and *The Impressions of Theophrastus Such.* Although in many ways disparate works, they nevertheless have a shared interest in examining forms of belief that are at odds with those enshrined in Eliot's realism – in particular ideas emerging from different branches of scientific enquiry that were having an increasing impact on Eliot's society.

Significantly, two of the works in the final group are also Eliot's last. One of the aims of this study is to trace changes between her early and late works. However, I will suggest that these variations are best accounted for, not necessarily in terms of Eliot's artistic development or increasing intellectual maturity, as they are usually conceived, but rather in terms of her choice of themes and subjects, and, moreover, her own changing intellectual context. Thus, for instance, we shall see that the complexities of *Daniel Deronda,* or indeed *Middlemarch,* can be explained, not as the products of a more mature and complex mind, but rather as responses to a changing environment, and an examination of a different set of issues. In order to explore these issues, the discussion is arranged so that the works are studied in roughly chronological order – with some exceptions.

In the first chapter, we will look at the two early works, *Scenes of Clerical Life* and *Adam Bede*, and compare these with her mature work, *Middlemarch*; in Chapter 2 we will examine the works of the middle years of her career: *Romola, Silas Marner, The Mill on the Floss, The Spanish Gypsy, Felix Holt*; and in Chapter 3 we will concentrate mainly on her late works.

A study of this length is necessarily selective, and I have directed my attention mainly to Eliot's fiction. It was as a novelist that George Eliot made her name (quite literally), but it was also, first and foremost, the way in which she characterized herself. Even though she keenly felt the prestige of other genres, especially poetry (she published a series of poetical works in later life), and toyed with the idea of drama (*Daniel Deronda* was originally conceived as a play), the genre of the novel seemed to offer her the perfect form in which to present her particular versions of the world. Her works mark an especially rich period in the history of that form, and suggest that there is some interesting coincidence between Eliot's intellectual project and the genre itself. Another aim of this study is to examine the ways in which the form set the parameters for her work, and, in a sense, determined the versions of reality that she could narrate, but also, conversely, in the later works in particular, the ways in which she would challenge the limits that the form imposed.

# 1

## Vague Dreams: Realism and the Drama of Details

'September 1856 made a new era in my life,' declared Eliot, 'for it was then I began to write Fiction' (*L.* ii. 406). In her journal entry of December 1857, she records how, gently encouraged by Lewes, she eventually drew out of the shadowy vagueness of her dreams her first piece of fiction, 'The Sad Fortunes of Amos Barton', the first of the three *Scenes of Clerical Life*. She continues:

> It had always been a vague dream of mine that some time or other I might write a novel, and my shadowy conception of what the novel was to be, varied, of course, from one epoch of my life to another.... I always thought I was deficient of dramatic power, both of construction and dialogue, but I felt I should be at my ease in the descriptive parts of a novel. My 'introductory chapter' was pure description though there were good materials in it for dramatic presentation. It happened to be among the papers I had with me in Germany and one evening at Berlin, something led me to read it to George. He was struck with it as a bit of concrete description, and it suggested to him the possibility of my being able to write a novel, though he distrusted – indeed disbelieved in, my possession of any dramatic power. Still, he began to think that I might as well try.... (*L.* ii. 406–7)

Striking in this description of her entrée to novel-writing is the emphasis that she places on *description* itself. 'Concrete description' came easily to her, more difficult to achieve was 'drama'. Lewes 'disbelieved in [her] possession of any dramatic power', but, he told her, 'You have wit, description, and philosophy – those go a good way towards the production of a novel. It is worthwhile for you to try the experiment' (*L.* ii. 407). The challenge for Eliot was to put the details drawn from her punctilious observations of life into a dramatic framework. In the end she was successful. Having settled upon a title and theme for her story – 'sketches drawn from my own observation of the Clergy' – she finally wrote a story so affecting, she later relates, that both Lewes and she 'cried over it' (*L.* ii. 408).

At the time she wrote the first chapter, the couple had just returned to their home in Richmond in Surrey from a trip to Tenby, where Lewes had been carrying out zoological research for his *Sea-side Studies.* In her account of how she came to write fiction, the emphasis on experimentation and, in particular, her method of writing from close observation from life lent her work a character similar to that of a piece of scientific research. Indeed, she approached her fiction in a scientific way; for each of the novels, she carried out thorough and painstaking research – her claim that description came easily to her belies the fact that it was produced through intensive labour. Moreover, she supplemented her observations of life with historical research, reading extensively from the literature of the period in which the novel was to be set. In preparation for *Adam Bede,* for instance, her first full-length novel, she read all the issues of the *Gentleman's Magazine* for 1799, the year in which most of the novel is set, taking copious notes on details as slight as the flora and fauna of the countryside, even the weather, so as to portray the scenes accurately. For *Romola,* set in fifteenth-century Florence, her researches in religious, social, and cultural history were so extensive and her pursuit of historical accuracy so dogged, that it almost paralysed her ability to write. She experienced bouts of headaches and depression, feelings of despair that she would ever be able to fashion from the details the substance of a plot. Lewes, always tactful, wrote to Blackwood, her publisher, advising him, when he saw Eliot, to tell her to 'discountenance the idea of a Romance being the product of an Encyclopaedia' (*GEB* 353).

Nevertheless, her labours were to good effect, for it is in her detail that she achieves a manner of providing descriptions that appear to bring the novels to life. Description holds the key to her realism. The material details of scenes and characters give them a solidity that makes them seem real and incontestable, so that the world of her fiction comes to resemble the recognizable natural world. So effective was Eliot's technique that her readers sometimes forgot that her novels were fiction. For many, they appeared to present records of the real world, specifically that of provincial England, that, as we discussed in the Introduction, inspired many of the most appreciative readings of her work. But Eliot's use of detail is, in fact, much more complex that this. Rather than providing an uncomplicated record of the way things really are, the material details are a means by which Eliot presents a constructed version of the way things may have been, or should have been. The details participate in the creation of the highly particularized world view that is implicit in all her works. Indeed, the details are always overdetermined, carrying a surplus of significance.

In this chapter we will examine her peculiar use of detail in her early and late works, the way in which she imbues elements of the material world with various kinds of significance and meaning. There are striking continuities in this respect throughout her œuvre, and in this chapter we will focus by way of example mainly, but not exclusively, on the early works, *Scenes of Clerical Life* (1858) and *Adam Bede* (1859), and the mature work, *Middlemarch* (1871–2). Paradoxically, material details are very often used to impart knowledge of things not usually visible to the human eye. For instance, a character's state of mind or motivation might be revealed through a detail of clothing, or an aspect of a room. Sometimes, such details are used to convey subtly some general authorial attitude or principle, or indeed a social or ideological meaning. Whichever way, the material details in the novels start to take on multiple lives, operating at a variety of different interpretative levels. Considered in this way, her novels shift from being documents of a materially substantial reality, to something more like a web or a tissue (to use Eliot's own metaphors) of intents and desires – more like a dream world than a real world. Indeed when we look more closely at her 'concrete description' it starts to dissolve back into the more shadowy world of values and judgements, and dreams and ambitions from which it came.

The opening paragraph of *Scenes of Clerical Life* presents an excellent example of Eliot's 'concrete description':

> Shepperton Church was a very different-looking building five-and-twenty years ago. To be sure, its substantial stone tower looks at you

> through its intelligent eye, the clock, with the friendly expression of former days; but in everything else what changes! Now there is a wide span of slate roof flanking the old steeple, the windows are tall and symmetrical; the outer doors are resplendent with oak-graining, the inner doors reverentially noiseless with a garment of red baize; and the walls, you are convinced, no lichen will ever again effect a settlement on – they are smooth and innutrient as the summit of the Rev. Amos Barton's head, after ten years of baldness and supererogatory soap. (*SC* 41)

There is almost too much description here, too many details. This kind of excess is typical of Eliot's style. The degree of attention paid to the church in this modernized state is surprising because, as we soon discover, the events of the story have happened twenty-five years beforehand. In fact this descriptive paragraph turns out to be, in a sense, superfluous, or 'supererogatory'[1] – like the Reverend's soap; if we are reading for the plot alone, we do not need to know about the church twenty-five years on.

Nevertheless it has a number of important effects. One is to persuade us that the place and the people really exist; not only do they 'live' in the time of the narrative, but they linger on, beyond the completion of the plot. Another is to make a contrast between the past and the present. The apparently excessive, or supererogatory, details of the modernized church function as a device through which the narrative can take stock of historical changes: the contrast between the old and the new church architecture comes to stand for a more general apprehension of the relationship between the past and the present. The details of the architecture thus perform as markers in a landscape of finely made judgements about the relative values of past and present. The wideness, smoothness, height, and regularity of the building are presented as signs of the church's new modernity, and opposed to a former, more irregular state in which Shepperton church was noted for 'its outer coat of rough stucco, its red-tiled roof, its heterogeneous windows patched with desultory bits of painted glass, and its little flight of steps with their wooden rail running up the outer wall, and leading to the school-children's gallery' (*SC* 41). This architectural randomness – this roughness and heterogeneity – is most striking in its difference from the new appearance of the church. Ironically, perhaps, the narrator confers an approval on the old church: the old church is picturesque; its irregularity lends it a certain charm, for which the narrator feels a 'sad fondness'. Indeed, the narrator even begins to identify with the architecture of the old church. 'Mine is not a well regulated mind', we are told; it, too, has the formal disorder characteristic of the old church. By contrast, the 'resplendent' and elegant new church is 'innutrient'. Its walls are so smooth and clean that not even lichen will grow on them. They are as smooth as the 'summit' of the Revd Barton's bald head. Through the description of the two church architectures, a clear set of values is presented in which the old is preferred to the new, the irregular to the regular, the modest to the openly august, and the intimate and untidy narrator to the bald-headed and overly scrubbed Revd Amos Barton.

In addition to their function as bearers of the text's authenticity, its realism, then, the supererogatory details of the architecture have a second role as signs of a value system that will operate within the text. In this value system, older, irregular things have precedence over new, ordered things – they are attributed a kind of organic life, which is compared with the sterile, 'innutrient', and, by implication, mechanistic quality of the modern. Moreover, the narrative itself will adopt the stylistic features of the old-style church: its own detailing of a kind of disordered, excessive materiality will confer a liveliness, an organic richness, on the scenes: it will, in a significant sense, bring the scenes to life.

The text is most effective when these two functions of material detailing coincide; when the details of objects, scenes, people that are included not only provide a sense of the irrefutable substantiality of the events, but at the same time signal certain value judgements that are upheld by the content of the narrative. Eliot's work is full of instances of this technique, which are characteristically quite complex. A number of good examples are provided by the uses that she makes of doors. In themselves, doors are an unremarkable aspect of architecture whose inclusion enhances the sense of the reality of the scene. But, as threshold points, doors also supply a wide range of symbolic possibilities. In *Silas Marner*, for instance, the miser's failure to lock his door initiates a series of events – the theft of his gold, the mysterious arrival of the golden-haired child, and his subsequent incorporation into the community – that constitutes his moral regeneration. In this case, the opening of the door represents the opening of his heart to the needs and desires of others, the awakening within him of his (up to then, latent) human capacity for sympathy. At other times, doors indicate points of indecision within the narrative, turning points that are crucial in the development of characters, and also, by extension, of plots. Eliot sometimes uses glass doors in this way: in *Felix Holt*, for instance, Esther significantly 'paused at the glass door' (*FH* 422) following her proposal from the morally flawed yet rich and attractive Harold Transome; in *Middlemarch*, Dorothea 'went out at the glass door' (*M.* 481) when struggling to answer her husband's, Mr Casaubon's unreasonable request that she carry out his wishes after his death. In both cases, the glass door suggests the characters' undecidedness – the fact that, metaphorically speaking, they could go either way. Other doors – not necessarily glass ones – offer commentary on the narrative processes on the text itself: open doors signal clarity, epistemological openness; closed doors a kind of opacity or knottiness. The passage from *Scenes of Clerical Life* cited above provides an example of this. The new church at Shepperton contains many doors – outer doors, inner doors, and, later, 'baize doors' – while the description of the old church remarks on none. That is not to say, of course, that the old church literally had no doors; but the failure of the narrative to note a door underlines the sense that the old church is somehow impenetrable, that it contains secrets, stories that will have to be prised out or broken into. It indicates a kind of complicatedness, a difficulty in the building that will be repeated in the text itself – a difficulty, moreover, that in a certain sense is the precondition for the text (if the story were 'open', it would not require telling).

This example demonstrates the way in which doors slip easily between their double functions as literal doors and figurative or metaphorical ones. This is a characteristic slippage in Eliot's work that happens so frequently that we barely notice it. For instance, in *Romola*, Romola's father, the blind scholar, Bardo, expresses his wish that his extensive library be preserved for posterity in terms that draw attention to doors: he wishes 'that [his] name should be over the door – that men should own themselves debtors to the Bardi Library in Florence' (*R.* 103–4). Ominously, his speech is interrupted when his servant, Maso, 'opened the door', announcing the arrival of 'the Greek scholar', Tito, the confidence trickster, who will be responsible for the loss of the library. The two doors mentioned here are, of course, literally doors; the idea that the name of the proprietor should be inscribed above the outer door is offered as a detail of historical fact made much mention of in the novel, and which contributes to the strong sense of fifteenth-century Florentine life. But there is also a figurative usage of the doors, and it is this that gives the passage its force and dramatic effect. The first door is a metonym for the library: it stands for the library (the collection of books) in a substitution made possible by the door's association with, its physical closeness to, the books. But, substituting for the books, the door also underlines the fact that the library belongs to Bardi, is in his possession. He develops the figure further, comparing his library to a bank and his books to money, for scholars who read in his library will be 'indebted' to him. When the second door opens (which may even be the same door as the first) for Tito to be announced, we are made well aware that Bardi's hopes for his library will be in vain – for doors can be opened by anyone, despite the name over the door. The 'indebtedness' that he had hoped for will come to nothing, the library will be dispersed, his legacy will be dissipated. In this way, the doors subtly open questions about inheritance and property that are central to the text as a whole. One message that the text imparts concerns the responsibility of inheritance, a responsibility ruefully lacking in Tito; for property requires familial protection by descendants or offspring that is firmer and more deliberate than merely writing over the door.

Positioned on the boundary between the exterior and interior, doors tend to mark the possibility of enclosure, which is the condition for private property. It is perhaps for this reason that Eliot's texts seem to admit a preference for closed doors – or, at least, doors that *can* be closed, or, better still, locked. When Mr Brooke, the irresponsible landlord and Radical parliamentary candidate in *Middlemarch*, is criticized for his neglect of his tenants' cottages, it is his failure to repair the doors and gates that is mentioned. His niece's husband, Sir James Chetham, agrees: 'Well, that is really a hit about the gates.' He continues,

'Dagley [a tenant] complained to me the other day that he hadn't got a decent gate on his farm. Garth has invented a new pattern of gate – I do wish you'd try it' (*M.* 383). Brooke's failure to protect the thresholds of his tenants' homes stands for his neglect of their general well-being, and is a sign of his failure to honour his paternalistic responsibilities as a landlord. Caleb Garth, by contrast, recognizes the importance of thresholds, that by properly maintaining the boundaries of interior and exterior one protects not only the domestic space, but also the family, and private property – both in the particular and as an institution. As critics continually note, there is a strong ideological content in Eliot's fiction which is very much in evidence in passages like this. A set of related terms – domesticity, private property, individual self-determination, and communal responsibility – receive constant approbation, and even become benchmarks of reality. Characters like Brooke who offend against these values are strongly criticized; in fact, their offence *is* their critique. This attack on Brooke comes in the context of a complaint that his charity does not begin at home, as in the Victorian truism, but instead 'increases directly as the square of the distance' (*M.* 383); like many reformers of the time, he is criticized for being in a sense long-sighted (as opposed to Casaubon, who is characteristically myopic), diverting his attention away from home, to distant, perhaps foreign causes.[2] By indicating that he has failed to repair his tenants' doors, the text makes it clear that Mr Brooke would allow the values of the domestic to be dissipated, while he attends instead to foreign markets. 'I've not always stayed at home,' he boasts in his ill-fated election speech. 'I've been in the Levant, where some of your Middlemarch goods go – and then again in the Baltic' (*M.* 504).

On the whole, the ideological investments of Eliot's work assume that it is better to stay at home than to travel abroad; if charity begins at home, so do personal happiness and fulfilment, and, by extension, the well-being of the local community. Characters who travel abroad on business – like Brooke, or Harold Transome in *Felix Holt* – tend to be morally flawed, while those who watch over and maintain homes – often looking after their very infrastructures, like Garth, or Adam Bede – are much ennobled.[3] Throughout Eliot's work, 'home' presents the very conditions for and the basis of social order itself. It encompasses a nexus of ideas that includes the concept of the family, and a set of social relations based on mutual need and cooperation, but also a location – in most cases in provincial England – and an economic base – usually traditional and land-based, rather than urban or industrial. This association with the land is very important, for it implies that the society that Eliot prefers is, in a sense, *grounded* in nature, just as the family, which provides the basic social unit, is perceived as natural and biologically given. Her ideal society gains considerable authority from these associations, as a permanent and natural or *organic* society, in contrast to new societies based on industrial wealth, perceived as being unnatural, or mechanical.

Through presenting this cluster of ideas – home, family, England, nature – Eliot constructs a complex argument about the superiority of an 'organic' society over the new forms of society brought about by industrialization and economic expansion. In line with many other writers and thinkers of the time, Eliot was deeply attracted to the idea of the organic as the basis for a social theory. Put simply, organic theories held that society was best conceived as a natural organism.[4] We shall examine these at greater length in Chapter 2, in particular their roots in the new biological sciences that were gaining prestige at the time. At this point, however, it is sufficient to note that organic theories were attractive to intellectuals of the period partly because they offered particularly expressive terms in which to object to the changes in the economic and social structure wrought by industrialization.[5] In this period the machine, as the polar opposite of the organism, comes to stand for an inhumane and uninhabitable modern world. Organic theories tended not to be against all forms of change, however, but had implicit in them a notion of gradual change. The belief was that, at its best, society should be allowed to develop or grow like a plant, retaining the social values associated with a traditional society, but nevertheless incorporating technological innovation and economic change. As we shall see, Eliot's novels give imaginative form to these beliefs so successfully and seamlessly that it is easy to forget that she is not merely describing the natural world.

Her early novel, *Adam Bede*, provides the clearest example of this. In many ways this novel follows the traditional pattern of the

*Bildungsroman*, the education novel which was the dominant form that the genre took in its early days in the eighteenth century.[6] It traces the development, or moral education, of the central character, Adam Bede, from the decent, yet fundamentally immature young man to the mature hero. This development is witnessed partly in his transference of affections from the vain and silly Hetty, to the morally refined, selfless Dinah. But it is also evident in his economic rise, from artisan to entrepreneur and bourgeois: at the beginning of the novel he is a wage-earning carpenter, but by the end he is a self-employed small business-man, the owner of the timber yard at which he works. This rise in his social status is accomplished without any real disruption of the existing social order: even Arthur Donnithorne, the squire, disgraced for having seduced Hetty, is reincorporated into the community by the end of the novel. The plot encourages us to believe that Adam's social and economic rise is a natural one – as natural as his 'growth' into maturity.[7]

Alongside Adam's growth as an individual, we also witness a gradual change in the ordering of social space in the novel. While at the beginning, inside and outside appear to merge, over the course of the novel there is a gradual bolstering of the distinction between the exterior world and an inner, private domain of the family in the home. In this process, doors and thresholds play a discreet but significant role. In the opening chapter, 'The Workshop', we are introduced to Adam, his brother Seth, and three other workmen, engaged in the activity of constructing doors. The scene is described in idyllic terms:

> A scent of pine-wood from a tent-like pile of planks outside the open door mingled itself with the scent of the elder-bushes which were spreading their summer snow close to the open window opposite; the slanting sunbeams shone through the transparent shavings... and lit up the fine grain of the oak panelling which stood propped against the wall. (*AB* 49)

The open door and window which allow the delicious scents of the wood to come in suggest a merging of outside and inside, of nature and man's products, making the workplace a natural place. This appears to be the ideal state, but during the course of the novel we are made to recognize that the outside is not necessarily benign, that dangerous things can happen there –

Hetty's seduction and the murder of her child, for instance. The idea that outside places – woods in particular, such as the Grove where Hetty is seduced – are locations in which dangerous behaviour is licensed, is a traditional one; for instance, Shakespeare frequently makes use of it in his comedies – in *As You Like It*, for example, in which the main action of the play takes place in the topsy-turvy world of the Forest of Arden. Eliot is drawing on this familiar literary idea, but in *Adam Bede* she puts a particular slant on it: her emphasis is on the need to protect women and children from the dangers that are in the outside world, to assign them a place within an enclosed realm of the home, and, above all, to demarcate the home as the only appropriate place for the expression of feeling and sexual desire. In the course of the novel, then, nature and society are separated from each other, not by creating an entirely new social space, but curiously, in effect, by drawing nature inside; the home, then, is very much conceived of as the enclosure of nature, a context in which the impulses that are usually associated with nature – the impulses of children, or those of sexual desire – can be regulated. As part of this process, another, wilder and more alien nature is produced – but safely located in the hazy distance of Australia, whence Hetty is exiled as punishment for her crime, and where she in fact dies.

In the Epilogue, however, we return to Hayslope, to the scene of the opening episode, but this time, eight years on, the workshop has been 'shut up half an hour or more' and our attention is shifted instead to the domestic scene, 'the pleasant house with the buff walls and the soft grey thatch'; significantly it is the boundaries, the walls and roof of the house, that we notice, emphasizing the enclosed nature of the home.[8] A 'figure' – who turns out to be Dinah, now married to Adam – 'come[s] out of the house, and shading her eyes with her hands as she looks for something in the distance, for the rays that fall on her white borderless cap and her pale auburn hair are very dazzling'. Then 'she turns away from the sunlight and looks towards the door' (*AB* 581). The location of Dinah on the doorstep is very significant. She begins the novel as a methodist preacher, holding out-of-doors sermons (their outdoor locations are stressed recurrently). On marrying Adam she, in effect, *comes indoors* – is domesticated, no longer a preacher, but a wife and mother. In the novel, this is the sanctioned position of women. Dinah is here pictured in a position similar to two older women earlier in the novel, emphasizing the sense of tradition, her continuity with past generations: Adam's mother, Lisbeth, who, on her first appearance in the novel, is standing on her doorstep, 'looking out' (*AB* 83), also in expectation of Adam, and a servant called Dolly, who stands 'on the door stone' (*AB* 56) of the very house that Dinah and Adam now occupy, feeding some chickens. The similarity between the three scenes is underlined by the fact that all three occur in the evening sunshine. Adam, who is responsible for drawing Dinah in (although, significantly, in the very last sentence of the novel, it is *Dinah* who invites Adam to 'come in . . . and rest; it has been a hard day for thee' (*AB* 584) ), began the novel building a door; now he is finally the head of a house with his own door that encloses and protects his family from the dangers of the exterior world.

By contrast, Hetty, who falls pregnant by Arthur Donnithorne, is, in a sense, sent out of doors; she wanders around the countryside while pregnant, looking for Arthur, and her final punishment for killing her child is to be deported to Australia. We might also note that, on discovery of Hetty's crime, Adam declares that the blame is 'at his [Arthur's] door, not at hers. *He* taught her to deceive . . . Let 'em put *him* on his trial' (*AB* 455). The door here is used metaphorically as a term for guilt or responsibility: the crime was of his doing, and should be returned to his domain. (In fact Adam is quickly talked out of his desire for vengeance against Arthur expressed here: while Arthur is culpable in his transgressive relations with Hetty, the ultimate responsibility for the crime is seen by Adam to rest with Hetty alone. In general, the narrative appears to concur with Adam that Hetty's is, as he puts it, 'a sort of wrong that can never be made up for' (*AB* 584), and is of her own doing.) In the scenes leading up to Hetty's trial and during the trial itself, there is much mention of doors and thresholds. Various characters are seen entering doors (not exiting), as though to underline the distinction between those who can come into society, who are socially incorporable, and the deviant Hetty, who cannot. In the evidence given against her, Hetty is represented as leaving and going to the 'open space' where the child's corpse is discovered. The first witness, the woman with whom Hetty lodged just before the crime, makes heavy weather of doors and locks: 'I didn't go out at the shop door, but at the back door, which opens into a narrow alley.... I didn't fasten the door behind me: there was no lock: it was a latch with a bolt inside, and...I always went out at the shop door. But I thought there was no danger in leaving it unfastened...' (*AB* 478). Interestingly, Bartle Massey, who, with the Revd Irwine, comes to occupy the position of moral authority in this episode, during the trial scenes becomes something of a janitor, 'unfastening the door' (*AB* 466) for Irwine, and locking the door of the room in which he and Adam are staying so that Adam might rest (*AB* 467). Later, he observes, oddly apropos of nothing, 'That's a thing never happened to me before...to go out o' door with my spectacles on' (*AB* 472). The narrator tells us that this is indeed a *non sequitur*, designed to dispel Adam's agitation, but it also provides some cryptic commentary on the story itself: that it is inadvisable to go outside with your glasses on, when there are dangers for which you should be prepared.

Adam's education (his *Bildung*) within the novel, his development to maturity, coincides with this new management of space – the enclosure of the domestic realm, the home, as a private and safe place. The subtle emphasis that is placed on doors within the text draws attention to this spatial reordering, which, like Adam's development, is presented as an entirely natural process. Significantly this transformation of space entails the enclosure of Dinah too, so that she becomes almost a physical constituent of the home. By the Epilogue, she seems almost to fuse with the door from which she emerges, bathed in the 'dazzling' evening sunlight which obscures individual outlines.[9] In the opening paragraphs of the novel cited above, the door under construction is similarly 'lit up' by the afternoon 'slanting sunbeams': it is as though the narrative is complete when this natural spotlight on the door falls on Dinah too, so that the two entities are drawn together, incorporated even. Moreover, in the dazzling evening light, Dinah appears almost sanctified. Throughout the novel Dinah tends to be shrouded in bright lights, which we associate with spiritual transcendence, endorsing her role as a preacher, and spiritual custodian. Here, however, the religious intensity has been expanded to encompass the home too.

At the end of the novel, then, Eliot presents what for many Victorians would have been a picture of an ideal home: a special, sanctified place, a refuge from the threats of the external world. In this home, the wife occupies a privileged place, as loving aide and nurturer of the family, and, above all, the moral centre of the family. Recent critics have devoted a great deal of attention to this version of the family, which is identified as the central facet in what is known as Victorian domestic ideology. As feminist historians, such as Leonore Davidoff and Catherine Hall in *Family Fortunes*, have demonstrated, this ideology was crucial to the establishment and maintenance of a bourgeois sense of identity. The roles it ascribed to women are ambiguous and constraining, offering two mutually exclusive positions, as either the morally spotless and socially conforming figure, like Dinah, or the wicked and dangerous, transgressive woman, like Hetty.[10] In this ideology, the difference between the two types of woman is made most clear in the representation of their sexuality: if the good woman ever had sexual feelings, these are now incorporated into her overwhelming feelings of maternal love, for, above all, the good woman is a good mother; on the other hand, the bad woman is a sexualized woman, her sexual desires are disruptive of the entire social fabric. Critics have been surprised to find that Eliot, whose own domestic situation was very unconventional, should have subscribed to this ideology, but nevertheless *Adam Bede* appears to present a clear demonstration of its operations. The social relations presented in the novel, and, in particular, the way in which Hetty and Dinah are pitched against each other as agents of social disruption or sympathetic consolidation respectively, illustrate this. Thus when, in the Epilogue, Dinah 'looks towards the door' in her beatific way, the text underlines the fact that the domestic space, the home, in the course of the novel, has been established as the ground rock of the social order – the foundation of the ideal, organic society, which is fundamentally linked into the order of nature.

Through the use of details, such as the mundanities of doors, Eliot is able to present a complex picture of the world that attempts not only to portray an accurate, or at least a convincing, account of how things really are, but to portray it in a way that incorporates certain preferences. As we have seen, the details have a double function, as, on the one hand, a guarantee of the representation's authenticity, but also as a frame through which particular values can be imparted. Thus the doors in *Adam Bede* both provide testimony to the substantialness of the world of the novel, but also indicate patterns of social exclusion and inclusion, and participate in the construction of an ideal, organic social order. Their double function is never openly acknowledged, as the second tends to be absorbed into the first. The effect of this, of course, is to neutralize, or naturalize, the social values that are propounded. It is in this way that Eliot manages to present this particular world view as the only one – a picture of life as it really is.

In a famous narratorial intervention in *Adam Bede*, Eliot divides novelists into two groups: 'clever novelists' who are 'able to represent things as they never have been and never will be', and herself, modestly, 'obliged to creep servilely after nature and fact' (*AB* 221). Of course, the drift of the passage makes it clear that this evaluation of the two kinds of novel is disingenuous, for, in this context, the ability to document 'nature and fact' is the superior one in all kinds of ways. Later she tells us that 'Falsehood is so easy, truth so difficult' (*AB* 222), underlining the moral investment in documentation: it is in fact more *difficult* to write the truth, despite the cleverness of the novelists who, in effect, tell lies. In the end, the truthful, realist novelist is the cleverer, and indeed the more committed: her regard for authenticity confers on her role a certain social responsibility, authority, and power. By emphasizing so strongly the moral and social purpose of documentation *per se*, and by underplaying her own imaginative input, the narrator subtly aggrandizes her own role; in her own account she is no less than an agent of the truth.

The narrative voice in Eliot's works tends always to assume this moral high ground, but it doesn't always take the same form. In *Scenes of Clerical Life* and again in her last work, *The Impressions of Theophrastus Such* (1879), the narrator assumes the persona of an elderly cleric, travesting herself, a disorderly woman, into a home ideologist; but usually Eliot's narrators are nameless and faceless. In her early works she was concerned to conceal her own identity, so an elderly clergy man gave her a convenient mask for her to hide behind. Naturally, with the success of *Scenes of Clerical Life* and *Adam Bede* there was a great deal of speculation about the true identity of 'George Eliot'. The finely observed details of clerical life in the first work convinced many readers that 'George Eliot' was 'himself' a clergyman. Even members of Eliot's family and her close circle of friends were persuaded of this; resemblances of certain characters and places in the stories to those of their own acquaintance made them suspect that the writer was a cleric called Joseph Liggins, who had once lived in the neighbourhood.[11] Paradoxically, however, it was the very details that seemed to confirm her assumed persona that also began to give away her true identity. Thomas Carlyle, for instance, found that the material details of the description presented evidence of the writer's true sex. Coincidentally, it was the doors that did it. On reading the opening pages of *Adam Bede* he declared: 'I found out in the first two pages that it was a woman's writing – she supposed that in making a door, you last of all put in the *panels*!' (*GEB* 273)

Despite the somewhat sexist tenor of Carlyle's remark (why should he assume that all men would necessarily possess a knowledge of carpentry that all women would lack?), the observation is interesting because it points out that, in her supposedly objective and impersonal descriptions of the material worlds of her novels, Eliot could not help leaving traces of herself behind. While, on the one hand, her use of detail seems to be very controlled – as we have seen, she always makes good use of the symbolic potential of material details – there are also places at which the excesses of the details slip out of her reach, when the text reveals more, or less, than it means to. Here Carlyle picks up on a fundamental paradox within her work: that, in her attempts to be the truthful narrator, the objective teller of nature and fact, the very devices that she chooses to effect this aim reveal its impossibility: the thorough listing of the material details of the world – her concrete descriptions – are, in fact, literary devices, tokens staked to authenticate the existence of a world that is only ever an imagined one. What appears to be solid and certain is in fact chimerical: it is no more than the sign of the author's realist ambition, her wish to disguise her imagined world as a reflection of a substantial world. Once we recognize this, the provincial worlds of Shepperton, Hayslope, Treby Magna, even

Middlemarch, seem more like fantasy worlds, and the material details of their environments merely symptoms of the author's creative desires.

Perhaps in recognition of the difficulty of her task, Eliot provides various discursive frameworks in order to ground her realism. Frequently she uses visual metaphors, in which we, the readers, are very emphatically given the position of spectators, as though *seeing* will engender in us belief. These metaphors typically operate in fairly complex ways. For instance, in *Adam Bede* she chooses to compare her fiction with a certain kind of painting – the work of the Dutch school, which included artists such as Vermeer. In this type of work, the accurate depiction of the various objects of everyday life – flower pots, stone jugs, mob caps – confers authenticity upon the scenes represented. For Eliot, what is significant is not only that the paintings select scenes of unexceptional, everyday goings-on, among a lost social stratum, but that they uncompromisingly represent the ugliness and clumsiness of people – resisting a tendency to idealize appearances.[12] Eliot suggests that 'squat figures, ill-shapen nostrils, and dingy complexions' (*AB* 223) are the norm among British people, and should not be disguised in the telling of their stories. We should not be spared these 'vulgar details', for they become testaments to the humanity of her characters, assurances of their reality. And, being 'real', they can be the objects of our sympathy; as she puts it, 'a fibre of sympathy' will connect us with them. We not only believe in their reality, but are allowed to enter into human relationships with them. Through the metaphor of the painting, then, Eliot manages not only to authenticate the scenes that she presents in her novels, but also, in a sense, to bring them to life, by humanizing our relationship with them.

Later in the same novel, she complicates the visual metaphor further, by recognizing the role that the narrator plays in presenting particular scenes. Now she claims that she

> aspires to give no more than a faithful account of men and things as they have mirrored themselves in my mind. The mirror is doubtless defective; the outlines will sometimes be disturbed; the reflection faint or confused; but I feel as much bound to tell you, as precisely as I can, what that reflection is, as if I were in the witness-box narrating my experience on oath. (*AB* 221)

Here she draws on two conventional images for a realistic representation, the reflection in the mirror, and the legal testimony, to impute, not the accuracy of the representation (indeed, she admits that this is most likely flawed) but rather the reliability of the narrator. The idea of the mirror is one that has been used since ancient times to explain works of art that attempt to represent lived experience.[13] But Eliot knows that the mirror, as a device for ensuring the accuracy of the representation, is problematic – that its image, as she puts it, will always be a 'defective one' that distorts and frames its reflection. So she displaces the image – the mirror here is the narrator's mind, not the work of art: the deficiencies are located in the narrator, and become a sign of her (or his) fallibility and humanity. The legal image works similarly. The evidence may – indeed, will – contain human error, but we should not doubt the honesty of the narrator. Objectivity *per se* – servile creeping after 'nature and fact' – is no longer the aim; instead we are offered a juridical notion of the truth, in which facts are to be construed on the basis of evidence. The narrator-witness affirms her (or his) own trustworthiness, but is limited by the necessary partialness of human vision. In this court we, the readers, are the jury, with the task of weighing the evidence, but what is striking is that there is only one witness, one narrator, one source of evidence. The image of the witness box promises a discursive context in which various stories will be compared, weighed against each other, as in a court of law – as in the trial scene at the end of the novel; but it is a promise that it fails to deliver.[14] Here we have only one witness, and moreover, one that openly admits to being 'defective'.

The overall effect of this passage is, nevertheless, to persuade us, not that this is an accurate account of the events, but rather that the events are rooted in actuality, observed, as they have been, by this flawed, but nevertheless human, witness. It is a cunning strategy, for it achieves its aims by focusing on the presumed element of unreliability in the narrator: her (or his) fallibility is a testament to her humanity, and, by implication, therefore, the proof of the events' reality. The legal metaphor thus provides a more complex, and more convincing, account of the realist project than the ingenuous claim of 'servile creeping after fact and nature'. It suggests that we consider the narrative as detailed evidence from which the truth might be construed.

In the later novels other metaphors are invoked to support the realism of the texts, but ones which nevertheless similarly have recourse to acts of seeing. As J. Hillis Miller has observed, the gaze provides the primary metaphors with which Eliot underpins her realism, whether this be the aesthetic gaze of the spectator of paintings, or the juridical gaze of the witness.[15] In *Middlemarch,* it tends to be the scientific, or clinical, gaze that takes precedence. Middlemarch society is recurrently compared with organic structures – like webs or tissue – which we are invited to examine, with the narrator, in the manner of a scientist. The idea of tissue, in particular, lies at the centre of the particularly rich and intricate network of metaphors that dominate *Middlemarch.* On the one hand, it is presented as one of a number of fabric-like, woven materials that are recurrently invoked as metaphors for social relations. But, as we shall go on to explore in more detail at the end of this chapter, the medical idea of tissue provides the basis of a particular way of seeing that is at the very core of the novel's concerns.

As a metaphor for social relations, tissue (or the web or net) operates by suggesting that individuals are like the individual strands of a piece of fabric, which are woven together, inextricably bound in systems of mutual need and dependency. The metaphor describes the constituency of Middlemarch society – the way in which individuals are not only bound to the community, but also constitute the community in their relations with others. But it also describes the text itself, a *textile* in which the various strands of the narrative, the different plots, intermingle to provide the substance of the novel. The metaphor is an endlessly malleable one, transformed at different moments. At some points it describes the way in which individuals might be trapped by the exigencies of social relations or the egotistical demands of others. Rosamund, for instance, is frequently represented as a spinning creature, a spider, weaving a 'gossamer web' in which to entrap Lydgate. But Lydgate is also a spinner, frequently complicit with Rosamund's desires. He, too, 'fell to spinning that web from his inward self with wonderful rapidity', participating in the construction of the shining fabric of their romance, 'made of spontaneous beliefs and indefinable joys, yearnings of one life towards another, visions of completeness, indefinite trust' (*M.* 346). In this case, the web is an analogy for a relationship of mutual cooperation and love – in Eliot's terms, the laudable characteristics of human sympathy – but here the image also gives a sense of the insubstantiality of this, the fact that it is born of fantasy, and has no firm roots in reality. Lydgate's scientific research is described in similar terms. As he takes up the 'threads of investigation', he weaves a knowledge for healing that embodies his finest sympathetic feelings – 'the yearnings of one life towards another'. But in the same way as his romance with Rosamund is represented as being somewhat unrealistic, so is his commitment to the medical regeneration of society. As in his marriage, his vocation is made impossible by his failure to countenance the effects of the material interests of those less committed to the ideal community that is embodied in the image of the web. In this case, the very fragile nature of the web suggests that Lydgate's commitment is to a fantasy of social cooperation, rather than to real networks of material society.

In other contexts, the idea of the social web, of lives intermeshed to form the fabric of the ideal community, is invoked in a less equivocal way. Dorothea's struggle is resolved when she realizes that her life is 'bound up with another woman's life' (*M.* 787), that there are 'three lives whose contact with hers laid an obligation on her' (*M.* 788). It is not simply a recognition of others that is important here, but her sense of her duties in relation to others that are accrued through the interconnectedness of human endeavours. This recognition is followed by her vision of life 'beyond the entrance-gates' of Lowick:

> On the road there was a man with a bundle on his back and a woman carrying her baby; in the field she could see figures moving – perhaps the shepherd with his dog. Far off in the bending sky was the pearly light; and she felt the largeness of the world and the manifold wakings of men to labour and endurance. She was part of that involuntary, palpitating life, and would neither look out on it from her luxurious shelter as a mere spectator, nor hide her eyes in selfish complaining. (*M.* 788)

Dorothea's enlightenment here lies at the core of *Middlemarch*, and accords with the novel's moral project. It is a vision –

literally – of the ideal, organic society: men and women being and labouring, at one with the natural world. Her revelation is that she too has a part in this 'involuntary, palpitating life'. In this phrase, life itself is represented as a natural organism – a totalizing force that draws all individuals into its quivering domain.

The distinctly physiological terms here suggest that Dorothea's glimpse of 'involuntary, palpitating life' gives her something in common with Lydgate, another close observer of human life. Lydgate's medical research into the cellular structure of organic matter, or tissue, is described in great detail. He had been inspired by the work of the historical personage, the French physician, Xavier Bichat (1771–1802), one of the major figures in the medical revolution of the end of the eighteenth century that Michel Foucault has called 'the birth of the clinic'.[16] Through his painstaking studies of the details of the organs of dead bodies, Bichat had ascertained the notion that the matter that lay beneath the surface of the organism – that is, tissue – was fundamental to the body's well-being. For Bichat, Eliot explains, the living body must be understood as 'consisting of certain primary webs or tissues, out of which the various organs – brain, heart, lungs, and so on – are compacted' (*M.* 148). It is only through knowledge of the body's primary constituents, its tissue, that a true understanding of the body, 'its frailties... and repairs', can be reached. The web which, as we have already seen, provides Eliot with the model for an ideal society is also the basis of tissue, of matter – the very fabric of the natural body. In this analogical thinking, her conception of society is as natural as the human body.

The narrative assesses Bichat's discovery in optical terms as a kind of revelation or enlightenment: his work had the effect of 'the turning of gas-light... on a dim, oil-lit street, showing new connections and hitherto hidden facts of structure which must be taken into account in considering the symptoms of maladies and action of medicaments' (*M.* 148). Lydgate, who wished to extend Bichat's work further, to 'go beyond the consideration of the tissues as ultimate facts in the living organism' (*M.* 148) and isolate the constituents of tissue itself, is said to create 'another light, as of oxy-hydrogen, showing the very grain of things and revising all former explanations' (*M.* 148). These very precise optical images – the vision that is enhanced by the illuminations of the gaslight or the oxy-hydrogen light – through which to express the nature of these medical innovations is instructive, and part of an extended interest throughout the novel in instruments of seeing. As Foucault has explained, Bichat's significance lies as much in his techniques as in his discoveries – his special techniques of *looking*.[17] As all physicians of the time, Bichat was concerned with charting the details of the appearance of the body through close observation; but, unlike others, he looked *inside* the body, through dissection, at the very substance beneath the surface. Through his special techniques of dissection, Bichat penetrated into the interior of the body. According to Foucault, this penetrative, clinical gaze has an organizational, or *disciplinary*, function: it is the act of looking inside that organizes details into a particular structure and produces medical knowledge. In *Middlemarch*, this provides Eliot with a model for realism, for the novel is, like Lydgate's own research, a project inspired by Bichat. Thus the narrator's gaze penetrates beneath the surface of things, and organizes details into a structure and a meaning; but in *Middlemarch* the body to be analysed is not a physical one but a social one. Inspecting the small details of the interstices of provincial life, Eliot is able to diagnose the diseases or disorders of society.

The images of looking that dominate *Middlemarch* must, then, be understood in the context of the clinical gaze: the gaze of the expert, who looks inside and organizes details into knowledge. Foucault has suggested that this gaze not only defines medical science in this period, but also sets the terms for the relationship between patient and doctor that characterizes modern ideas of medical practice, in which the patient plays a passive role, his or her body displaying symptoms for the scrutiny of the all-knowing, and, in this context, all-powerful doctor. Moreover, the clinical gaze also describes the social relations that are typical of the modern, industrial society that is taking shape in this period, which are similarly characterized by an imbalance of knowledge and power between institutionally based, and increasingly centralized, experts, and the general mass of the population. Significantly, one of the most important themes of *Middlemarch* is the uneasy process of professionalization among doctors; Lydgate's modern ideas exasperate the existing medical practitioners of the town, whose very livelihood and prestige are threatened by the impact of his new kinds of techniques. Indeed, it is his support for the developing profession of forensic medicine – which, in fact, gained impetus from the findings of clinicians such as Bichat who developed the techniques of the post-mortem – that is one of the first causes for his alienation in the Middlemarch community. More generally, however, in its dissection and examination of the body of society, the narrative itself adopts the stance of a clinician such as Lydgate, and thereby participates in the very processes of modernization that Foucault has analysed in *The Birth of the Clinic.*

Thus modes of penetrative looking associated with the techniques of the new medical science appear to be presented with approval as a progressive means to the good health of the body social. For instance, there are numerous allusions to the possibility of sighting a life within a life, an interior happening, concealed to normal vision, that encapsulates the truth of being, in which the microscope, which had proved such an important instrument for the followers of Bichat, provides the basis for a range of metaphors in the novel. In this context, the ocular capacities of particular characters, as we have already noticed in relation to Mr Brooke, signify their potential for insight and understanding. Dorothea is one such character whose development is charted around the transformation of her vision. In her case, it is not that her eyesight improves – rather it is a case of her beginning to direct her gaze towards the proper objects. In the beginning Celia, with some justification, complains that Dorothea 'always see[s] what nobody else sees ... yet ... never see[s] what is quite plain' (*M.* 36). The problem here is that her vision is unworldly, fixed on objects that are beyond the material world, that enable her to mistake the ominous signs of Casaubon's fossilized form for the distinguished look of the philosopher, Locke. By the end of the novel, she has exchanged this kind of blindness for a more useful ability to see 'what nobody else sees'. This is a vision that is closer to that afforded by the microscope – an ability to see into the fabric of things, to recognize the fibres of social duty that link one body to another.

Paradoxically, Dorothea's transformed vision at the end of the novel is closer than Lydgate's to that of 'the great Seer', Bichat. In his research, Bichat, in fact, preferred to use the naked eye rather than the magnified vision afforded by the microscope – even though scientists who developed his approach, like Lydgate, used the microscope.[18] In fact, in the novel, the microscope becomes the centre of a complex critique of the increasing professionalization of science in which Lydgate, the most avowedly Bichatian character in the work, represents its negative aspects: its increasing separation from the real, material concerns of society, which in Lydgate is manifested as his egotism.[19] Thus, despite being a professional user of microscopes, Lydgate never achieves the ideal form of vision that the metaphor of the microscope provides elsewhere within the novel. Instead of fixing on material realities, he spins fantasies and dreams; at one stage, he even takes opium, the elixir of Romantic dreamers, in order to escape the problems confronting him. This emphasis on Lydgate's Romantic spirit, his impracticality and passionate idealism, makes him something of an anachronism in Middlemarch. He is certainly out of place, although the novel is not quite sure whether he is before his time (as an innovative scientist) or after it (as a Romantic idealist). In this he is surprisingly like Casaubon, whose fossil status, which is emphasized over and over again, also makes him a throwback to some previous form of life. Lydgate's flawed vision is also evident in his scientific project, his wish to extend *beyond* Bichat's 'consideration of the tissues as the ultimate facts in the living organism' (*M.* 148) to search instead for the origins of human life. This ambition betrays him as a Romantic overreacher, out of touch with the material basis of proper and responsible scientific endeavour.

The microscope provides Eliot with an excellent metaphor for a certain kind of penetrative vision and insight that is akin to the clinical gaze, with its attendant social relations that Foucault later analysed. But the fact that Eliot prefers to use the microscope as a metaphor – a way of describing a new capacity to see that comes *naturally* to Dorothea, without the use of the optical instrument – is extremely important. It suggests that Eliot wishes to *naturalize* this kind of vision, to say that it comes to particularly fine examples of human beings as an attribute of their superior moral standing. It emphatically diminishes the role of modern technology, exemplified by the *real*, rather than the metaphorical, use of the optical instrument. In this respect, instruments of technology, like the microscope, are presented as the signature of the new, industrial society, from which the novel can be seen to distance itself. Early on in the novel we are warned of the dangers of microscopes:

> Even with a microscope directed on a water-drop we find ourselves making interpretations which turn out to be rather coarse; for whereas under a weak lens you may seem to see a creature exhibiting an active voracity into which other smaller creatures actively play as if they were so many animated tax-pennies, a stronger lens reveals to you certain tiniest hairlets which make vortices for these victims while the swallower waits passively at his receipt of custom. *(M.* 59–60)

In this context, the microscope is not a corrective to 'coarse' interpretation, but merely a self-fulfilling device, by which an egotist sees what he or she wants. By analogy, Lydgate's scientific understanding, reached through the use of the microscope, may give him advanced medical powers, but it also means that he remains an egotist, blinded by the limits of his own expertise. In this respect, science is associated with social fragmentation rather than organic cohesion.

Ultimately, the novel maintains an ambiguous relation to the impact of science and technology. On the one hand, through the presentation of the flawed character of Lydgate, it implies a stern critique of the social implications of scientific research: the increasing specialization and technologization of medicine, alienating it from the human needs of communities. But, on the other hand, the novel positively embraces the insight afforded by the new techniques of Bichat. As we have seen, the realism in *Middlemarch* is underpinned by the idea of the clinical gaze. The novel describes a society in the process of adapting to the transformations in social relations that are characterized by this new, penetrative way of looking, and, in a measured way, the very character of the realism in the novel duplicates its form. The element of critique within the novel is thus carried out from a fairly compromised position, in which the narrative attempts to distance itself from the very terms in which it has established its own project. In the end, we could say that in *Middlemarch* Eliot is both the clinician, participating in the creation of the structures of modern society, an agent of its transformations, but also its critic, regretting what she identifies as the dehumanizing impact of technological change.

Some critics see this ambivalence as an example of the text undermining itself in an unsettling way – the text's *deconstruction*.[20] For others, however, it can be read as a kind of pragmatism, which for some is the novel's greatest achievement: the presentation of a mixture of measured commitment to change, combined with a humanist scepticism – a recipe well suited to the leisurely and expansive form of the novel. Whichever way one views it, the important point to bear in mind is the complexity of Eliot's mode of representation in this novel as an accretion of different and contrasting points of view, or frames of reference: in this case, that of the experimental scientist, the modernizing clinician, as opposed to that of its critic, the organic traditionalist, speaking on behalf of continuity in social practices and relations. Consequently we have a sense of dialogue between opposing points of view in the novel, and one which, interestingly, there is no compulsion for us to see resolved. At best we could say that the novel adopts the position of a reserved progressive, or a sceptical traditionalist.

Within *Middlemarch*, then, it is possible to discern layers within the fabric of representation which give the text a sense of depth which corresponds to the kinds of imagery that the novel calls on. As we have noticed in this chapter, there is a strong strain of continuity between Eliot's early and late works in the selection of visual imagery as a means through which to organize the material details of the world in the presentation of 'concrete description'. However, in *Scenes of Clerical Life* and *Adam Bede*, these images came from modes of observation that attended to the exteriors of things, through the ideas of painting and legal evidence. In the later work, *Middlemarch*, she has adopted instead a set of metaphors from clinical medicine that are to do with looking inside. These metaphors give the work a sense of 'depth' that was lacking in earlier novels. If we were to identify a change between the early and late works we might characterize it as a shift from surface to depth, from detailing exteriors to interiors. This introduces a new complexity into her work in a way that seems appropriate to the mature works of a writer. However, we might also read this 'maturity' in other ways. For instance, in *Middlemarch* the sense of 'depth' is achieved through

Eliot's wish to interrogate a new way of understanding the world, a new way of organizing its details, that is characteristic of the scientific project that (following Foucault) is associated with modern forms of social organization. That is to say that this 'depth' is not necessarily a consequence of the maturing of the writer, but rather of a choice of a different subject matter and a different frame of reference. Moreover, this 'depth' ultimately allows Eliot to maintain an ambivalent position, poised between tradition and modernity, reserving judgement as to the benefits of either. In this case, 'maturity' could also be read as indecision or ambivalence. Interestingly, in her subsequent works, as we shall see in Chapter 3, this kind of ambivalence is no longer a comfortable characteristic of the realist-pragmatist, but is transformed into a radical symptom of modernity.

In the middle period of her writing career, from 1860 to 1866, in which she published four major novels, Eliot adopts a position that is closer to that of *Middlemarch.* In all of these works she documents the slow but steady march of progress, examining its social benefits and its costs. Nevertheless, as we have already noticed, the work of documentation is much more complicated than she would have us believe. This is particularly the case when social change is the subject of documentation. In the next chapter we will address the ways in which Eliot approaches the challenge of representing change. The phrase 'concrete description' that she used to characterize one aspect of her work in the journal extract 'How I came to write fiction', cited at the beginning of this chapter, implies a static object of representation. But Eliot comes to develop a form of representation that she would identify as 'organic' rather than 'concrete'. In the following chapter, then, we will examine this 'organic' form of representation in the works from *The Mill on the Floss* to *Felix Holt*.

# 2

# Regeneration: The Uses of the Family

In her private life, as in her fiction, George Eliot was much concerned with the idea of the family. Her own experience of families was a markedly unusual one: her mother had died when she was only 16; she had split dramatically from her father at the age of 23,[1] and, on her liaison with Lewes, she was disowned by her brother, Isaac. Moreover, Lewes, with whom she cohabited, had a family by his first wife in which the children were not in every case fathered by him. Latterly Eliot married John Cross, a man whom she was accustomed to call 'Nephew'. Despite all this, or possibly because of it, her correspondence reveals a particular desire to cast other relationships into a familial mould. She assumed a motherly role in relation to Lewes's sons and their wives, and 'adopted' a stream of admiring younger women whom she called her 'spiritual daughters' – Emilia Pattison, Edith Simcox, and Elma Stuart, whose grave, next to Eliot's in Highgate Cemetery, bears the inscription: 'one who for 8½ blessed years George Eliot called by the sweet name of "Daughter"'.[2] A self-styled mother, she signed her letters 'Mutter', 'Madre', 'Mother', 'Your loving mother (in the spirit)'.[3]

As a woman who had no children of her own,[4] this invention of herself in the maternal role is particularly striking. Around the time of the fatal illness of one of Lewes's sons, she wrote a letter to Emilia Pattison saying that she 'profoundly rejoice[d] that [she] never brought a child into the world', but, she went on to say, she was 'conscious of having an unused stock of motherly tenderness, which sometimes overflows, but not without discrimination' (*L.* v. 52–3). This Wordsworthian construction –

an 'overflow' of powerful feeling, which, in his 'Preface to the *Lyrical Ballads*', the poet had held to be the provocation to poetry[5] – has led some critics to assume that Eliot's excess of 'motherly tenderness' lay behind the production of her fiction. In this account, her novels take the place of her babies, putting to good use her 'unused stock' of maternal feeling. Such a reading is backed up by Eliot's own estimation of the importance that her relationship with Lewes held in the production of her work: it is as though her novels are the babies that the couple never had. 'But for the happiness his love has conferred on my life', she wrote in the dedication of *Adam Bede*, the work 'would never have been written'.[6] Eliot repeatedly represented her writing as taking place within a domestic and specifically marital context; in so doing, she concealed the decidedly irregular nature of her own circumstances. The idea of the conventional family thus appears to perform a particular function within her own self-representations, even though it bears little relationship to her experience. It suggests that her fictional families may well play similarly complex roles.

In the previous chapter we began to see the way in which the novels present the enclosure of the family space, the domestic interior, as a place of safety from dangerous incursions from the outside world. In this chapter we will consider the family's operations as an organizing theme in other of her writings. Eliot explores the idea of the family in all her works, without exception, although here we will concentrate attention on *Romola, The Mill on the Floss, Silas Marner, Felix Holt,* and *The Spanish Gypsy.* Not surprisingly, perhaps, biographers have suggested that her dramatization of the pyschodynamics of the family in her fiction was spurred by her own traumatic experience, and that the novels might be read as either representations of her own troubled life, or, more interestingly, as a kind of private therapy – a way of resolving her own personal conflicts.[7]

Eliot was not, however, the only person at the time to have suffered from family problems; nor was she, by any means, the only writer to explore them. Indeed, when we read more widely in the works of the period, it is clear that the idea of the family was a widespread Victorian preoccupation. In the writings of the time, the family emerges in a variety of ways: as a privileged site of personal experience, or as a social institution, or, in a more abstract way, as a model for society, or a bond between the past and the future. Here we shall investigate the ways in which Eliot's fictions draw on some of these versions of the family that were in circulation. The families that she represents in her fictions, we shall see, are composites, informed by motifs and ideas taken from a variety of different arenas – in particular philosophical, scientific, and social and political thought. This does not mean that they were not also influenced by her own special experience, but it does mean that they were framed by a much broader cultural context than studies that emphasize the biographical record would hold. Eliot's fictional families are more than a record of her private experience; they are carefully constructed interventions into some of the most important social and cultural debates of the time.

In Eliot's fictional families, the mother is the most important figure. In 'Janet's Repentance', for instance, she extols the virtues of motherhood:

> Mighty is the force of motherhood!... It transforms all things by its vital heat: it turns timidity into fierce courage, and dreadless defiance into tremulous submission; it turns thoughtlessness into foresight, and yet stills all anxiety into calm content; it makes selfishness become self-denial, and gives even to hard vanity the glance of admiring love. Yes; if Janet had been a mother, she might have been saved from much sin, and therefore from much of her sorrow. (*SC* 239)

Here maternal love is described as though it were an alchemical power, able to change negative human attributes into their opposites. The emphasis in this example is on the power of such love to transform the woman: Janet would have been redeemed if she had been a mother. In fact, during the course of the narrative she does experience something akin to maternal love, in relation not to a child, but to Mr Tryan, the evangelical preacher, of whom she takes care as he is dying of tuberculosis. For Eliot, maternal love is 'the essence of real human love' (*AB* 477); it is the ability to 'feel with another' (*SC* 229). In this description 'maternal love' bears close resemblance to Eliot's concept of sympathy, which is perhaps the most important term in her moral scheme. Eliot's understanding of 'sympathy' owes much to the work of the philosophers Spinoza and Feuerbach, by whom she had been heavily influenced. Feuerbach writes in *The Essence of Christianity,* a work that Eliot translated in 1854, 'My fellow man is the bond between me and the world. I am, and I feel myself, dependent on the world, because I first feel myself dependent on other men' (*EC* 82). He goes on to say that it is other men that transform the world from a 'dead and empty' place, to a 'meaning[ful]' one. What distinguishes men from lower forms of life is their ability to recognize that they are part of a larger group, a species – or a 'species being'; it is this recognition that allows a man to 'put himself in the place of another' (*EC* 4) – the act of substitution that is the basis of sympathetic love. Feuerbach writes at length about his notion of love as a strangely palpable, material thing – 'a real love, a love which has flesh and blood, which vibrates as an almighty force through all living' (*EC* 48).

Motherhood offers an ideal model for the concept of sympathetic love because of the close physical relationship that is shared between mother and child: in the beginning, the mother literally holds one life within another, her child's within her own. And it is this initial shared life that provides a model for all future relations with the child. She alludes to this process in *Adam Bede,* a novel in which styles of mothering are of central concern, when she writes that 'the mother's yearning, that completest type of the life in another life which is the essence of real human love, feels the presence of the cherished child even in the debased, degraded man' (*AB* 477). The image is a startling one, for here it is used to describe Adam's feelings for Hetty at her trial for the murder of her child. Adam is given the position of the mother, and Hetty, his former fiancée, his child. Within the narrative, this marks the high point of Adam's moral development, the moment at which he accedes to emotional maturity. In the confusion of relations and genders, one thing is quite clear: for Eliot the role of the mother is an emotional and possibly a practical one too, but it is *not* a biological one, for anyone can perform it, even men – even though, as we shall see later on, the potential for reproduction and regeneration are crucial to the symbolic power of the mother figure. To that extent then, the idea of the mother is something like a metaphor in Eliot's work – a metaphor for ideal human love.

Thus it is interesting to note that, in Eliot's works, most of her important central female characters are not in fact mothers – at least not within the main body of the narratives: Dinah in *Adam Bede* and Dorothea in *Middlemarch* have children only within the final chapter of each novel, Gwendolen in *Daniel Deronda* purposefully decides that she will not have children, and Romola has none of her own, despite her extreme maternal feelings. Moreover, neither Esther (in *Felix Holt*), Dorothea, nor Romola has a mother of her own. Eppie in *Silas Marner* is abandoned by her mother, as are, to all intents and purposes, Daniel Deronda and Tito (in *Romola*). Despite Eliot's sustained interest in mothering, the biological mother tends to be a strangely absent figure in the novels.

Of all Eliot's women, the childless Romola presents the most striking profile of the mother figure. Having been betrayed by her husband, Tito, she leaves the warring factions of Florence and drifts in a boat down a river hoping for death. Instead of her own death, however, she awakens in the midst of others' deaths, in a village infected with the plague by the recent arrival of Jews fleeing the Spanish Inquisition. Romola herself has undergone a kind of rebirth: the water had been for her 'the gentle lulling cradle of a new life' (*R.* 641). There is a mythic quality to the scene: here Romola is like Moses, an abandoned child, who, like the prophet, will found a community and a new order. But the idea that the water provides a kind of womb from which she can, in effect, be *mothered* is also important and suggests a particular reworking of the Moses myth. Previously we have been told that Romola experiences her predicament as though she had been 'orphaned': 'Had she anything like the dream of her girlhood? No. Memories hung upon her like the weight of broken wings that could never be lifted – memories of human sympathy which even in its pains leaves a thirst that the Great Mother has no milk to still' (*R.* 590). During the course of her sleep, her 'dreams of her girlhood had really come back to her' (*R.* 640–1). Restored in this way, remembering her own mother's love for her, she is able to perform as a mother towards the few remaining living villagers she meets – first a small Jewish baby, then a woman, then a Christian youth. The sympathetic love that she demonstrates is described specifically in terms of maternal love, available to her because it is remembered, passed on between mothers and daughters. (Memory is very important in *Romola;* it offers a means of maintaining tradition and continuity within a personal history at a time of massive social and political disruption.) In this scene, pictured partly through the eyes of the Christian youth who observes her actions, Romola's maternal love is given a religious significance, for she is represented as the Madonna, administering to the remnants of life among the corpses. The narrative draws attention to the composition of the scheme as though it were a painting, as it assumes the iconography of religious representations of the Virgin. Here Eliot presents the scene in terms of a tableau vivant, a technique that she adopts at many symbolic moments within her texts:[8] 'With her gaze fixed intently on the distant slope, the long lines of her thick grey garment giving a gliding character to her rapid walk, her hair rolling backward and illuminated on the left side by the sun-rays, the little olive baby on her right arm now looking out with jet black eyes, she might well startle that youth of fifteen, accustomed to swing the censer in the presence of a Madonna less fair and marvellous than this' (*R.* 644). More marvellous than the Virgin Mary, Romola literally changes the 'dead and empty' place into a living one through nursing the sick.

In the novel, Romola is continually compared with Tito's childish mistress, the pretty Tessa, whose silliness – and fecundity – are stressed throughout. At the end Romola 'adopts' Tessa and her two children, acting as the 'Great Mother' for this new family. The idea of the mother, then, is associated not with biological regeneration but rather with the social role of nurturing. This is a learned (or remembered) and cultured role, not a biological function. By contrast, the instincts of a 'brute mother [who] shields her young from the attack of the hereditary enemy' (*R.* 152) are associated with Tito, as a way of denoting his selfish desire for self-preservation. A somewhat confusing array of qualities are associated with Tito. He is frequently compared with animals, like the 'brute mother', or 'a fleet, soft-coated, dark-eyed animal' (*R.* 106), someone with 'animal spirits' (*R.* 185), highlighting the dominance of his instincts, that he behaves in unreasoned, animalistic ways. However, he is also associated with extreme rationalism; through most of the novel Tito is a cold strategist, cunningly planning the steps to his own ascendancy. In this respect he is sometimes compared with a machine: 'a machine with complex action' for instance, 'leaving deposits quite distinct from the line of talk' (*R.* 166). Although seemingly contradictory, both the animal and the machine images suggest that his behaviour is somehow inhuman – less than human, or mechanical, like an automaton – and make a clear contrast with the humane and sympathetic behaviour of Romola.

Interestingly the comparison is encapsulated in a set of images that suggest that, as an antithesis to Romola, the mother, Tito is a child *murderer*. Early in the narrative, when the extent of Tito's evil is only just becoming apparent, we are told that 'our deeds are like children that are born to us; they live and act apart from our own will. Nay, children may be strangled, but deeds never: they have an indestructive life both in and out of our consciousness; and that dreadful vitality of deeds was pressing hard on Tito for the first time' (*R.* 219). Expressed here is a general point about the impossibility of avoiding the consequences of one's own actions. But the extremity of the idea – that deeds are in fact more tenacious than children, who can at least be strangled – is shocking; under this pressure, for people such as Tito at least, child murder becomes almost expedient. Thus it is less surprising to discover later that 'he had never yet done an act of murderous cruelty even to the smallest animal that could utter a cry, but at that moment he would have been capable of treading the breath from a smiling child for the sake of his own safety' (*R.* 422). In both cases, the murder of an infant is presented as the most extreme act of self-interest, what Eliot would term 'egoism' – the precise opposite of sympathetic love. Here, however, child murder, like maternity, is offered as a metaphor rather than an actuality. In the novel Tito shows no inclination really to murder children, his own or others – no more than Romola bears children of her own; indeed, it is a parricidal desire, to kill his stepfather (interestingly, not a blood relation either), that overwhelms Tito in the latter parts of the text. But his repeated connection with metaphors of infanticide is as significant as Romola's with maternal ones. In fact one early reviewer compared Tito with Hetty Sorrel in *Adam Bede*: '[Tito] is Hetty,' he wrote, 'but a man, and not a fool.'[9] In both cases these egotistical characters work against the constitution of the organic society: Hetty and Tito must be expelled or repressed in order for the harmonious ending to be achieved. And in both *Adam Bede* and *Romola* the harmony that is established at the end is organized around the regenerative unit of the family, at the centre of which is the mother.

In both novels the family that is constituted at the end represents the epitome of cultured or civilized life. This is a particularly important point to note, because most of Eliot's novels – particularly her earlier ones – tend to tell stories that are fundamentally concerned with the transformation of a society from an earlier, less civil state, to an improved, cultured state. The novels thus generally stage progressive versions of history, in which the family operates as the basis for the new society. *Romola* follows this trajectory most clearly. Set in Renaissance Florence in the 1490s, the novel documents a period of exceptional change, a time that could be considered as being at the cusp of modernity. The drama of these fictional characters – Tito, Romola, Bardi, Tessa – is set amidst the doings of real historical characters and the turmoil of real historical events – the expulsion of the Medici, the invasion by Charles VIII of France, and the rise and fall of Savonarola. The major theme of the novel is to consider how individuals deal with historical change, which, within the course of the narrative, is represented as an ineffable force; how individuals might shape, from the changing circumstances of their time, the conditions for a better society. Romola is seen as shifting allegiances from her father, who represents Renaissance learning and culture, to join Savonarola, the religious fanatic who attacked the materialism and paganism of Renaissance culture, only to opt finally for a compromise between the values of religion and art, suggested in her allusions to both Savonarola and the artist, Piero, in the final chapter. Such a compromise gives her access to humanitarian values of sympathy, located in the newly constituted family, as against the self-destructive egoism of Tito. In this way she manages to draw together social and personal duties. Indeed, as many critics have pointed out, there are many correspondences between the dilemmas represented in *Romola* and the contradictions that Eliot herself had experienced within her own lifetime.

The idea that civilization advanced in this progressive way was widely held by intellectuals of the time and propounded by the thinkers most influential to Eliot. Feuerbach, for instance, proposes a progressive history in *The Essence of Christianity*, in which he traces social development from an early stage, characterized by the emphasis on religious belief, to a more advanced stage in which the ideal being, or God, is held to be a projection of an ideal version of man – the species being. For Feuerbach the most advanced form of civilization is the one in which Christian belief has been displaced by a belief in the divinity of the human form. Many other nineteenth-century thinkers proposed versions of this progressive understanding of history that were particularly influential for Eliot, including Darwin, whom we shall discuss later, and the French positivist thinker, Auguste Comte. Comte held that civilization had passed through three stages: the theological stage, in which men explained the world through their belief in gods and spirits; the metaphysical stage, in which notions of essences and abstractions were drawn on; and finally the positivist stage. The positivist stage, in which society now found itself, was the most advanced point of civilization; knowledge was now grounded in science, and was always relative to men's social and material conditions.[10]

Such progressive theories of history provide a useful context in which to understand the dominant theme in *Romola*: the emergence of a state of civilization from a state of barbarism. In fact, as we shall see, the novel provides a complex and ironic account of such a process. Much attention is paid to modes of behaviour, or manners, that constitute civilized behaviour, as opposed to the rough, uncultured behaviour of 'brutes'. For instance, shaving presents an early opportunity for discussing the distinction between the brutalizing, barbarous conditions of hirsute men, and their civilized, shaved, 'human' state. Here Nello, the barber, becomes an agent of civility. Maggie Tulliver's disastrous haircut in *The Mill on the Floss* provides the opportunity for similar kinds of reflections. The latter novel is also centrally concerned with the processes of civilization, but here the focus is on the education of children, from behaving impulsively, like 'the lower animals', to becoming 'members of a highly civilised society' (*MF 91*). In *Romola*, however, the highly civilized politicians and courtiers are shown to be scheming and in fact over-civilized, sly and manipulative – and thus, ironically, barbaric. Tito is the supreme statesman; his diplomacy is admired through much of the novel – but eventually his statecraft transposes into a raw savagery. One of the courtiers, Tornabuoni, remarks tellingly, 'we have that power of concealment and finesse, without which a rational cultivated man, instead of having any prerogative, is really at a disadvantage compared with a wild bull or a savage. But, except yourself [Tito], I know of no one else on whom we could rely for the necessary discretion' (*R.* 417). In this absurd hierarchy of civility, the 'rational cultivated man' needs the added 'power of concealment and finesse' to make him a match for a savage. But Tito exceeds even this. The shadowy presence of the historical figure, the arch-schemer Machiavelli, on the peripheries of the narrative, underscores the point that the values of civility are ultimately self-serving and debasing. Instead the novel endorses the humane values of Romola – 'having wide thoughts, and much feeling for the rest of the world as well as ourselves' (*R.* 674) – as the epitome of civilized, cultured society. Thus, during the course of the novel, the definitions of civil and savage behaviour are redrawn and, in the end, come to revolve around the idea of the family. The community that Romola founds within her constructed family at the end of the novel constitutes both the locus and the model for cultured life. On the other hand, Tito's associations with child murdering – a frequently used sign of the barbarian – seal his savagery and also his fate: as a throwback to some former, less civilized era, Tito's destiny is extinction in this newly modernized, humane world.

The family occupies an important place in all Eliot's works. As in *Romola*, it supplies the ideal conditions in which people are able to live in relations of mutual love and sympathy, and provides a model of social relations that could be extended to the whole of society. In fact the idea of the family was widely used in political discourse of the time as a privileged model for social organization. For instance, conservative writers such as Carlyle drew on an analogy between the family and society in their prescriptions for a paternalistic form of government in which the working class were to be looked after like children. That Eliot's fiction shares much with such neo-feudal thinkers is evidenced in the most overtly political of her novels, *Felix Holt*. However, unlike writers who emphasized the patriarchal role of the father as the linchpin of the unit, Eliot's works present an array of variously flawed father figures: the fanatically litigious Mr Tulliver in *The Mill on the Floss*, the muddle-headed and unreliable Mr Brooke in *Middlemarch*, the physically and mentally degenerate Mr Transome and Harold's natural father, slippery Jermyn in *Felix Holt*. In *Silas Marner*, one of the few positive portrayals of fathering, the surrogate father-figure seems to be more maternal than paternal: he offers his adopted daughter nurture and comfort, but fails hopelessly as a disciplinarian. On the whole, Eliot's rendition of the family is one that is far more sympathetic to the idea of strong and substantial female figures than the more usually represented Victorian patriarchal family in which women occupy the position of morally pure, but otherwise sweet and decorous doormats.

Apart from its uses as a model for ideal social relations, the family, as a generative unit, also provides Eliot with a pattern for gradual social change. Through the production of new generations, the family creates a future within a framework of continuity and stability. Such a model of incremental social change was very attractive to Eliot, who, as we have seen, was committed to ideas of social progress when these respected the perceived organic structure of society. In this model, the woman's role as a mother is crucial. Even though Eliot insists that the maternal role is a social rather than a biological one, nevertheless it is the idea of the mother, her child-bearing potential, that gives the family its special character as a place of regeneration. The emphasis that she lays on maternity – even when, paradoxically, mother figures, like Romola, do not have their own children – is best understood in this context: the mother, as a reproducer, both inaugurates change and maintains the continuities of family inheritance.

Eliot's use of the family as a social model very much reflects the fact that she was writing at a time when the dominant intellectual models were organic ones. As historians of ideas have shown us, later eighteenth- and nineteenth-century European culture witnessed a displacement of the mechanical model as an explanation for natural and social phenomena by a biological one. For instance, Enlightenment thinkers followed Descartes, Harvey, and the scientific revolution in thinking of the world, and by extension the workings of the human body, in terms of a machine. Many held that society, too, would be best organized along mechanical principles, and the French Revolution of 1789 provided the opportunity to put mechanical social laws into operation. Critics of the Revolution, such as Edmund Burke writing in his *Reflections on the Revolution in France* (1790), focused precisely on what he called, pejoratively, this 'mechanical philosophy', blaming it for the violence and social disorder he perceived the Revolution to have brought about. For Burke, society was better conceived of as an organism – a plant or a body; his *Reflections* abound with extended metaphors of a somewhat eclectic collection of plants and animals – oak trees, cattle, grasshoppers. For him the organic was preferable to the mechanistic social model because it determined that all change should be gradual, bound by a sense of a natural process, and that the maintenance of tradition and continuity, and traditional social hierarchies, should be a guard against abrupt social change.

One reason why the metaphor of the organism became a popular one at this point was the change taking place in the biological sciences and, in particular, embryology. Until the middle of the eighteenth century most scientists held to the preformation theory, in which the embryo was generally considered to have contained within it in a miniature version of all the characteristics of the fully formed individual. The German scientist Caspar Friedrich Wolff revolutionized the understanding of foetal development by introducing a theory of 'epigenesis'; in his work *Theoria Generationis* (1759) he argued that, rather than merely growing from small to large, the embryo is subject to a process of differentiation and change, developing from a simple to a complex form. Anatomy textbooks from the nineteenth century provide a useful demonstration of this interest in the dynamic process of growth, for we find in them page upon page of illustrations of the minute changes in the development of the embryo: the development of the limbs, the growth of facial features, the formation of internal organs, even the stages of development of the genitals.[11] As Sally Shuttleworth explains, the new embryological theory 'made it possible to explain change not as a movement towards chaos, but as a movement towards a higher state of order'.[12] Moreover, she goes on, the effect of the new theory was to shift the understanding of growth 'away from the visible surface of nature and towards the historical process'. Thus it is easy to see how the new understanding of embryology was in tune with the later development of evolutionary sciences, which similarly understood organisms to be subject to constant processes of development, in these cases, striving to adapt to the ever-changing circumstances of their environments. Both embry-ology and evolutionism focused attention squarely on the necessity of historical process, and, by implication, also provoked a reconceptualization of the relationship between the individual and those processes of historical change.

The centrality of the science of embryology to the development of organic theories helps to explain why the family (the social location of biological reproduction), and in particular the mother (its physical location), should hold such symbolic power within Eliot's work. Both occupy a central place in a process of development, which for Eliot is fundamentally inexorable, beyond the control of individuals or institutions – like her notion of historical change that we have seen represented in *Romola*. The family and the mother thus stand as symbolic guardians of the grand processes of biological, and, by extension, historical development. In the face of this, individuals have only the power gained from their accommodation to its relentless processes, but possess no autonomous capacity for change.

Significantly, Eliot uses an embryological metaphor in *Middlemarch* to confirm the position of individuals within the larger scheme of things. Contrasting Will Ladislaw's realistic sense of his own potential with Casaubon's blindness to the futility of his academic endeavours, the narrator comments ironically: 'We know what a masquerade all development is, and what effective shapes may be disguised in helpless embryos. – In fact, the world is full of hopeful analogies and handsome dubious eggs called possibilities' (*M.* 83). The embryological image here provides the means for disposing of the superstitious belief that we might see into the future by predicting our fortunes from pictures of our present – as in the preformation theory. It is not that the progress of events is not already determined; the point is that their order is not immediately visible. Will Ladislaw, who is invoked in this passage, knows that, and uses scientific observation as the basis for ordering his own life. For instance, we are told that 'Will saw clearly enough the pitiable instances of long incubation producing no chick...'; in this case, Mr Casaubon provides the 'pitiable' evidence of fruitless incubation that will provoke Will into action. Eliot's world is fundamentally an ordered one, determined by natural laws; in it, those who are able to adapt to that order – on the basis of scientific knowledge gained through experience and careful observation – are the individuals who are destined for success. Science thus offers Eliot metaphors for conceptualizing the proper place of the individual within the larger processes of history. At best, individuals, like Will, are able to adapt to the demands of their own environment. Those who cannot are represented through evolutionary metaphors as fossils; Casaubon in *Middlemarch* and Bardi in *Romola* are good examples of characters whose intellectual and cultural allegiances are with a past generation, and who as a consequence are represented as being on course for extinction.

Within Eliot's evolutionary scheme, the ability of the individual to adapt to his or her particular environment is vital for survival. But for Eliot, some environments are more conducive to human accommodation than others. As most commentators of her work have noted, she demonstrates a clear preference for rural, provincial settings over urban, industrial centres. Such environments tend to provide the conditions in which the ideal social relations of mutual love and dependence that are achieved during the course of the novel (such as those epitomized by the relations between Romola and her adopted family) are able to flourish. In line with many other writers of her period, Eliot usually presents patterns of imagery in which organic, natural things and processes are opposed to mechanical, manufactured ones. In this world view, the organic tends to be associated with the pre-industrial.

In *Silas Marner*, for instance, Silas, an 'emigrant... from town into the country', rejected from Lantern Yard, a 'hidden world' within an urban, industrial context, moves to the pastoral haven of Raveloe, with its 'orchards looking lazy with neglected plenty; the large church in the wide churchyard, which men gazed at lounging at their own doors in servicetime; the purple faced farmers jogging along the lanes or running in at the Rainbow' (*SM* 63). The plot tells the story of Silas's adaptation to and gradual incorporation into his new environment, brought about through the arrival of the golden-haired child, Eppie, and the constitution of his 'family'. Curiously, and somewhat anachronistically, urban society and industrial or mechanized labour are consistently figured in evolutionary terms as processes that are subject to change and extinction, while Raveloe, by contrast, is presented as a permanent, unchanging environment. By the end of the narrative, Lantern Yard is indeed 'extinct': when Silas returns there at the end of the novel to clear his name of the crime of which he was wrongly accused, the place has disappeared without trace, replaced by the architecture of yet newer forms of industrial production, the factory. In the early stages of the novel, Silas, too, is associated with this state of near extinction. He is a 'remnant of a disinherited race' (*SM* 51), his strangeness described in terms that draw together mechanized labour, religious fanaticism (Lantern Yard is an evangelical sect of the kind that is historically associated with emergent industrial communities) and primitive life forms. The word 'remnant' is very noticeably repeated throughout the early stages of the novel. Silas is frequently compared with a spider, the creature held by the evolutionists to be the oldest extant species, a 'spinning insect', weaving from 'pure impulse, without reflection', doing repetitive, mechanical labour that dispels his consciousness, and gives him 'a mechanical relation to the objects of his life' (*SM* 69). His mechanized weaving loom, brought with him from Lantern Yard, is a sign of his difference from the other inhabitants of Raveloe; it has a 'questionable sound', in sharp contrast to the 'natural' machines of agricultural labour. Moreover, he is subject to fits, which make his body appear to be dead – but also mechanical, with a 'mysterious rigidity and suspension of consciousness' (*SM* 56): in Lantern Yard these fits were associated with religious ecstasy, for which '[t]o have sought a medical explanation . . . would have been held . . . a wilful self-exclusion from the spiritual significance that might lie therein' (*SM* 56); but later in the story they are understood to be a medical condition, cataleptic fits. During the novel, he will be, metaphorically, coaxed back to life, his body made organic, less rigid and mechanical, within the 'natural' society of Raveloe. As in *Romola*, the closing image of *Silas Marner* is that of a newly constituted family – 'four united people' (*SM* 244) – Silas, Eppie, her new husband and mother-in-law – approaching their home, an organic, garden idyll. Significantly, this is Silas's old house, indicating permanence and continuity, but expanded to accommodate his larger family, and it is 'fenced with stones on two sides, but in front there was an open fence, through which the flowers shone with answering gladness'. Even the plants here are in perfect harmony with human happiness. 'O father,' says Eppie in the closing sentence, 'what a pretty home ours is! I think nobody could be happier than we are' (*SM* 244).

While *Silas Marner* tells a story of a community gradually adapting itself to its organic conditions, *The Mill on the Floss*, on the other hand, tells of an organic community becoming extinct, shattered by the processes of modernization. In some ways this is the most conservative of Eliot's novels – or perhaps merely the most pessimistic of them – in that it charts the tragic inability of the community and individual characters in St Oggs to adapt to the inexorable changes of history. The deaths by drowning of Maggie and Tom at the end of *The Mill on the Floss* are potent symbols of the defeat of their family in the face of the unstoppable forces of natural or evolutionary change. *The Mill on the Floss* is seeped in allusions to evolutionary science, and each example tends to convey a sense of the failure of individuals to adapt to their circumstances. The people of St Oggs, we are told, constitute 'a kind of population out of keeping with the earth on which they live – with this rich plain where the great river flows for ever onward, and links the small pulse of the old English town with the beating of the world's mighty heart' (*MF* 363). And we would be wrong to think that the River Floss might represent an unchanging natural force. As Jules Law has pointed out, the river too is subject to the changes of a modernizing world, for it is in fact the new technologies of irrigation that bring about Tulliver's ruin.[13] According to Law, the river stands for the uncertainty of the future in a world that is subject to the consequences of technological change. Tulliver, unable to adapt to the impact of technological development in irrigation methods, is cruelly disabused of his belief that 'the rights and wrongs of water' are 'plain enough', that 'a river's a river, and if you've got a mill, you must have water to turn it... Pivart's erigation [*sic*] and nonsense won't stop my wheel'

(*MF* 226). Both the Tullivers and the Dodsons are described in terms of 'races' who are too *traditional,* believing in the continuity of things, and living out the lives of those of generations before them. For example, Mr Tulliver's grandfather 'was descended from one Ralph Tulliver, a wonderfully clever fellow, who had ruined himself' (*MF* 365), in the same way that Mr Tulliver will do in this novel. This sense of tradition, in which their lives repeat those of generations before them, is not a bad thing. Indeed, it is often this that provides the basis for sympathetic relations: for instance, Mr Tulliver treats his sister with compassion on the mistaken grounds that his behaviour towards her will determine his son, Tom's, treatment of Maggie. The problem in this novel is that such traditional beliefs pay no attention to the changing circumstances in which characters find themselves, or the fact that each generation is not, contrary to Tulliver's belief, determined by the actions of the previous one. Indeed, the narrative speaks of the 'onward tendency of human beings [to rise] above the mental level of the generation before them, to which they have been nevertheless tied by the strongest fibres of their hearts' (*MF* 363). This unavoidable splitting of emotional bonds under the onward force of historical development is the subject of the novel. *The Mill on the Floss* tells the story of what happens when generations and environments become out of step with each other, when the family is displaced by material conditions that will no longer accommodate it.

The social philosophy evident in Eliot's fiction is illuminated by an early essay that she published in the *Westminster Review,* entitled 'The Natural History of German Life' (1856). This is a review essay of the work of Wilhelm Heinrich von Riehl, the German physiologist-turned-social scientist whose works were important in the establishment of the new discipline of sociology in Germany. His idea was that a society might have a 'natural history', as though it were a collection of plants or animals; thus it would be possible to examine the present, modern state of society as though it were the result of a long process of development.[14] Eliot's essay on Riehl is an approving one, and many of her views expressed here have been taken by critics as statements about her own subsequent work as a novelist. She writes of the weightiness of Riehl's sociological project in much the same terms that she describes the work of realist fiction: she alludes to the 'sacredness' and 'seriousness' of his task, which is, tellingly, to 'paint... the life of the People' (*E.* 110). She approves of Riehl's work because he assumes, with her, that 'the People' will be accurately represented only when they are examined in their 'natural' circumstances. By 'natural' circumstances, they both appear to mean a traditional, land-based and pre-industrial environment – what we might call an organic environment. The German peasantry that Riehl describes presents a privileged case history because the lives which peasants lead are informed by customs and beliefs that have developed over many generations; they live in the same places and engage in the same occupations, and, as people who live and work on the land, these are customs which have been developed through a repetitive and productive interaction with the land and natural processes. Riehl's German peasants show a marked resemblance to Wordsworth's peasants, famously described in his 'Preface to the *Lyrical Ballads*'. For both writers, the peasant's relationship with his 'natural' circumstances is thus a special one, because his circumstances are in a particular sense 'natural', and the organic integrity between the peasant and his environment allows the peasant to become an extension of the natural world in which he lives. As critics have noticed, this description of the peasant appears to lie behind many of Eliot's fictional characters – Adam Bede and Felix Holt, for instance, seem to be embodiments of the finest qualities of such traditional, rooted people,

But what of people who do not live in these kinds of 'natural' circumstances – those who live in cities, who work in factories, whose customs and beliefs have not passed through many generations? If accurate documentation requires the people to be described in their 'natural' circumstances, how will it be possible accurately to paint the lives of those transients or émigrés who live in alien or 'unnatural' circumstances? How could they be represented with the integrity that both Riehl and Eliot demand? The problem here is implicit in Eliot's account of Riehl's larger project, which is to 'urge on the consideration of his country men, a social policy founded on the special study of people as they are – on the natural history of the various social ranks' (*E.* 129) – but it is never finally resolved. Eliot favourably contrasts Riehl's method with that of 'socialists', by which she probably had in mind figures such as Engels, Marx, or Fourier, who

> have thrown themselves with enthusiastic zeal into the study at least of one social group, namely, the factory operatives; and here lies the secret of their partial success. But unfortunately, they have made this special study of a single fragment of society the basis of a theory which quietly substitutes for the small group of Parisian proletaires or English factory-workers, the society of all Europe – nay, of the whole world. (*E.* 129)

Riehl's sensitivity to the variety of human experiences, and his awareness of the need for analytical models that are responsive to the special conditions of particular lives, by contrast, leads him to the conclusion that *'a universal social policy has no validity except on paper'* (*E.* 130) – a point with which Eliot concurs so strongly that she italicizes it. Throughout the essay Eliot expresses a profound dislike of theoretical knowledge which, following Burke and Carlyle, she conceptualizes as a mechanization of knowledge, associated with industrial production and the varieties of alienation it is considered to confer. On the other hand, a kind of knowledge that is gained through engagement with the material particularities of individual lives is conceptualized as organic knowledge; it is associated with the integrity and wholeness of human individuals, and, by extension, with community, a healthy body politic, with country locations, and traditional forms of society. There is a striking circularity in the argument here. Despite the declared sensitivity to the need for analytical models alive to the particularities of different experiences, this very sensitivity itself is the basis for a model of knowledge that strongly privileges one kind of social organization over another: pre-industrial, so-called organic societies over modern, industrial, urban societies. In this analysis, the organic model is one that tends towards stasis. It is unable to provide Eliot with a way of conceptualizing historical change, for, in this account, the very notion of change is associated with the mechanical model.

To a certain extent, a solution to this impasse is offered by the family – or rather the possibility of biological reproduction within the family, which will allow the amalgamation of country and city folk. As the 'emotional susceptibility', 'nervous diseases', and headaches of modern, urban life are unknown to the peasant who lives in the healthy environment of his birth place, Eliot, following Riehl, offers the striking idea of intermingling of stock, the mixing of breeds, as a remedy against the physical degeneration incurred by modern life: 'Happily, many of the younger sons in peasant families, by going to seek their living in the towns, carry their hardy nervous systems to amalgamate with the overwrought nerves of our town population, and refresh them with a little rude vigour' (*E.* 120). Through the intermarriage of townswomen and peasantry the population will be bolstered, strengthened by this influx of hardier stock. Here we see a literalizing of the metaphorical uses of the family that we have observed elsewhere in Eliot's work. In *Silas Marner*, for instance, the 'overwrought' and nervous body of Silas is 'refreshed' by a figurative, rather than a sexual, regeneration within the family. In the example in the essay, however, it is the very physical process of reproduction that brings about a social regeneration. The idea of racial amalgamation, the mixed family, thus provides a useful model of social change.

The image of interbreeding is a particularly striking one – especially as Eliot was writing at a time of heightened concern about racial mixing. Anthropological debates throughout the period centred on the issue of whether or not the races were in fact different species, as was held in polygenist theories, or whether they were varieties of the same species or family, the view of monogenists. The debates were morally and politically charged; they were staged in a context behind which lingered the powerful arguments of the anti-slavery campaigners whose rhetoric revolved around the notion of an inclusive family of mankind, as opposed to those who believed the Negro to belong to a different species from the white man. As Robert Young has explained in *Colonial Desire*, racial theorists of the mid-nineteenth century concentrated attention on the offspring of mixed racial unions to support their beliefs: some held that such offspring were physically weak and morally degenerate, physically unable to reproduce themselves, and liable to extinction; others argued that amalgamations embodied a positive mixing of qualities, and that, indeed, all races were in fact fusions of 'pure' breeds; while others adopted a middle position, and held that amalgamation between some 'proximate' races was possible and desirable, but between more 'distant' races was impossible.[15] That Eliot was familiar with these debates is clear not only from our knowledge of her friendship and association with many of its key players – Herbert Spencer, for instance, and Charles Darwin and Francis Galton – but also from issues that emerge in her writings. These receive fullest treatment in her last novel in relation to the future of the Jew, Daniel Deronda, but they also appear in the earlier works with some persistency. I will return to *Daniel Deronda* in the final chapter, but here it is useful to note the way in which the idea of the amalgam – the cross-breed – is evoked in her earlier works.

There are many instances of 'cross-breeds' in her works. Adam Bede, for instance, is strikingly described in terms of his mixed racial origins: '[i]n his tall stalwartness', we are told, 'he was a Saxon'; but his 'jet-black hair' and 'dark eyes that shone from under strongly marked, prominent, and mobile eye-brows, indicated a mixture of Celtic blood' (*AB* 50). As Young points out, by the middle of the century, the predominant notion of Englishness was one that emphasized a racial mix – a mixing of Saxon and Norman, or, as here, of Saxon and Celt – in order to differentiate an English identity from the racially pure Teutons. Adam Bede's mixed origins indicate that he is the ideal English type. A less English type – but nevertheless an embodiment of a positive, vital racial fusion, is Will Ladislaw, in *Middlemarch*. His origins – part English, part Polish, part Jew – although scorned by members of the upper-class Middlemarch set, determine his role within the narrative as a regenerating force. Interestingly, like Adam Bede, the marks of his racial ancestory are evident on his body. For instance, much is made of his profile, the bump in his nose, that recalls his grandmother, Casaubon's Aunt Julia, and puts into place the genealogical connections that are vital to the plot. But the bump on the nose also indicates his potential for adaptation and change: 'the little ripple in his nose', we are told, 'was a preparation for metamorphosis' (*M.* 209). In line with the novel's commitment to ideas of evolutionary change, Ladislaw is thus identified as a character with a dynamic future, a potent trajectory, in strong contrast to the fossil, the pure-bred Casaubon.

Another character who is referred to as a cross-breed is Maggie Tulliver in *The Mill on the Floss*. Maggie is not exactly a racial mix, but her mixture of two families of different temperament and economic status, the Tullivers and the Dobsons, is constantly represented *as though it were* a mix of races – 'the crossing o' breeds', as her father puts it (*MF* 59). As for Adam Bede and Will Ladislaw, Maggie's mixture places her on the side of the future – it is a sign of her capacity for positive change. However, unlike these other characters, Maggie inhabits a world that cannot acknowledge her potential for change: the environment of St Oggs is one that has atrophied, stuck in an uncompromising commitment to tradition. Rather than being marked out as someone who is adaptable to new environments, like Adam or Will, Maggie is destined to advance beyond her circumstances, to become fatally out of step with her time.

The fact that Maggie is a woman is significant. Indeed, her father accounts for her social difficulties in precisely these terms. She's '[t]oo 'cute for a woman... an over 'cute woman's no better nor a long-tailed sheep – she'll fetch none the bigger price for it' (*MF* 59–60). Her cleverness is compared with the characteristic tail of a special breed of sheep – a decorative adornment, superfluous to market value. But if female intelligence is construed as an eccentricity of evolution, female stupidity is equally anachronistic. The other women of St Oggs are represented as belonging to a primitive species. For instance Aunt Pullet is humourously displayed in a state of grief:

> It is a pathetic sight and a striking example of the complexity introduced into the emotions by a high state of civilisation – the sight of a fashionably drest female in grief. From the sorrow of a Hottentot to that of a woman in large buckram sleeves, with several bracelets on each arm, an architectural bonnet, and delicate ribbon-strings – what a long series of gradations! (*MF* 111–12)

The long description of Aunt Pullet quietly sobbing that follows is openly parodic, and the comparison with a Hottentot woman raises the idea that, rather than being different, the woman in the 'high state of civilisation' is equally primitive. The novel suggests that women of this rural community are in fact anthropological throwbacks, prevented by their environment from proceeding to a higher stage of development. Indeed, it is the fashionable attributes of modern life (the 'buckram sleeves' and 'architectural bonnet') that accentuate the unreasonableness of innate female emotional response. Maggie's intellectual and social ambitions, however, position her in advance of other females in the community, but no more advantageously. Throughout we are told repeatedly that her restless spirit would be more easily understood if she were a boy; that society could countenance a force for change if its source were masculine rather than feminine. Interestingly, her aberrant adventurous spirit is represented in terms that also imply racial difference. Especially in the early parts of the novel, there are constant references to the brownness of her skin, and her primitive, animal-like behaviour; she is frequently compared with a gypsy – a connection that is highlighted when she in fact runs away to a gypsy camp. When she does join the gypsies, she embarks on a comical attempt to teach them to read and write in an ill-fated attempt to 'civilise' them. At this point, Maggie's difference from the gypsies is as clear as is her difference from the primitive society of St Oggs. Her own mixed, or amalgamated, condition separates her from both the gypsies and the primitive women of St Oggs. Through mixing the codes of race and gender, Eliot implies that the education and social advancement of women are natural parts of the evolutionary process, but ones that are very slow and cannot be hurried by the acts of precocious individuals like Maggie.

In a letter addressed to her friend, John Sibree,[16] dated March 1848, Eliot lays out some of her ideas about race that are explored further in her fiction. The letter is full of bravado, clearly meant to make an impression, and differs from her more mature views, explored in particular in *Daniel Deronda*. Nevertheless it is important to bear in mind that Eliot is voicing opinions that were at one with those of many anthropologists and scientists of the time. The point that comes over clearly in this letter, which illuminates her treatment of race in her fiction, is her preference for racial 'fusions':

> Extermination up to a certain point seems to be the law for the inferior races...for the rest, fusion both for physical and moral ends. It appears to me that the law by which privileged classes degenerate from continual intermarriage must act on a larger scale in deteriorating whole races. The nations have always been kept apart until they have sufficiently developed their idiosyncrasies and then some great revolutionary force has been called into action by which the genius of

> a particular nation becomes a portion of the common mind of humanity. Looking at the matter aesthetically, our ideal of beauty is never formed on the characteristics of a single race. I confess the types of the 'pure races', however handsome, always impress me disagreeably – there is an undefined feeling that I am looking not at man but a specimen of an order under Cuvier's class, Bimana. (*L.* i. 246)

At this stage, for Eliot, purity of race is indicative of a kind of primitive state, like 'Cuvier's class, Bimana', the one-handed life form, which is morally degenerate and aesthetically disagreeable. Pure races, such as gypsies or Hottentots, are evolutionary remnants, spectres of a receding and inglorious past. Racial amalgamations, on the other hand, are buoyant and strong, launched into a trajectory of moral improvement and social progress. Distasteful as such racial thinking might be, it nevertheless provides something of a framework for many of Eliot's earlier works.[17]

It is in the relatively late work, *Felix Holt*, however, that Eliot interrogates these ideas of inbreeds and amalgams most carefully. As in *The Mill on the Floss*, in which Eliot used beliefs underpinned by contemporary racial theory to explain the position of men and women in society, in this work she uses racial theory to express ideas not only about races but also about class – a key issue in a novel which is ostensibly about the Reform Act of 1832. The old gentry family, the Transomes, is in a state of degenerative decline: Mr Transome is an elderly imbecile; his first son is already dead as a result of mental and moral decline induced by generations of inbreeding. Harold Transome – the son on whom hopes for the economic rejuvenation of the estate rest – is revealed in the course of the novel to be the offspring of an illicit affair between Mrs Transome and the lawyer Jermyn. In this case, the mixing of blood between classes makes him a stronger individual both physically and, in the end, morally, although his moral redemption remains more questionable than his physical strength. Harold Transome's mixture of gentry and middle-class origins draws on racial theories of the amalgam to present the idea that a mixture of adjacent types brings about a positive strengthening. But the novel also includes a character who is a much more extreme mix: Harold's 'half-breed' son, the young 'oriental' who accompanies him on his return from Smyrna. In this case, the mixture of distant races makes the child as degenerate as the inbred Englishman. Throughout the novel this child is represented as a savage, who finds a soulmate in the elder Mr Transome – the two romping through the house as though they were animals. Like Darwin and other racial theorists of the time, Eliot presents the view that breeding between 'distant' races ultimately leads to the same kind of physical and mental degeneration as inbreeding: races should 'fuse', but the difference between them should be strictly managed – not too close, not too distant. As an analogy to the political situation, this theory of race thus provides Eliot with a strong justification for the restricted extent of parliamentary reform that was achieved in 1832, when the franchise was extended only to middle-class men: adjacent classes should and must mix, but the culturally and socially distant working class should remain separate and distinct. There is a sense in which the mixed-race child functions as an analogy for the possibility of the enfranchisement of the working class – a disruption that cannot be considered within the limits of this novel.

At various moments the horror at the idea of the radically mixed child erupts, as violently as the rioting workers at another stage in the novel. For instance, towards the end, when the heroine, Esther Lyons, is being wooed by Harold Transome, the narrator records the following interchange between them in which the child's parentage is openly discussed for the first and last time.

> 'You don't suppose, I hope, that any other woman has ever held the place that you could hold in my life?'
>
> Esther began to tremble a little, as she always did when the love talk between them seemed to be getting serious. She only gave the rather stumbling answer, 'How so?'
>
> 'Harry's mother had been a slave – was bought, in fact.'
>
> It was impossible for Harold to preconceive the effect this had on Esther. His natural disqualification for judging of a girl's feelings was heightened by the blinding effect of an exclusive object – which was to assure her that her own place was peculiar and supreme. Hitherto Esther's acquaintance with Oriental love was derived chiefly from Byronic poems, and this had not sufficed to adjust her mind to a new story, where the Giaour concerned was giving her his arm. She was unable to speak; and Harold went on –

> 'Though I am close on thirty-five, I never met with a woman at all like you before.' (*FH* 421)

This is the sole substantial reference to a former wife whose shadowy existence – confirmed only in the material form of a 'savage' and exotically dark son – contributes to the air of eastern mystery that surrounds Harold on his return to England after the years spent in Smyrna. Hitherto, the mystery of the child's parentage has not been probed too deeply – merely accepted by his family and the inhabitants of Treby as an ingredient in the peculiar concoction of differences that constitute Harold Transome's alienation from his own roots: he had 'come from the East, was as rich as a Jew, and called himself a Radical; characteristics all equally vague in the minds of various excellent ratepayers' (*FH* 194). The narrative lays clues as to how we should interpret the passage: Harold's change of taste in women from the dark slave to the fair and (relatively) free European woman marks a stage in the moral development of his character, and Esther's realization of the inadequacy of Byronic literature as an aid to understanding the world marks a stage in hers. Moreover, Harold's inability 'to preconceive the effect this had on Esther' suggests that differences between them are irreconcilable, and warns us that a union between them might prove to be impossible. But the passage also conceals things from us. We are not told, for instance, what the effect of the revelation is on Esther. She was 'unable to speak', was 'still silent', and finally, after more confessions on Harold's part, closes the conversation. What Harold could not 'preconceive', *we* are not allowed to conceive. Moreover, we are told nothing more about the marriage itself: the interesting details of courtship (or purchase), union, and his wife's subsequent death – details that make the common substance of all Eliot's plots and which would be all the more interesting in the case of marriage to a slave. What remains striking about this passage is that the shocking revelation of the former wife's enslavement is dropped as quickly as it has emerged, and is left more or less uninterrogated in a narrative that characteristically dwells on the smallest of details.[18]

The incomprehensibility of this event is significant because it underlines, in a negative way, a point that is at the heart of *Felix Holt*: the importance of precedents. If Harold has 'never met a woman like Esther before', Esther has certainly never met a man like Harold. For Esther, as well as for us, the shock of a man who has been married to a slave is, above all, the shock of the new. On the whole the novel prefers to return to things that it already knows, and finds things for which there are no precedents variously unsettling. Esther, therefore, will turn down Harold and the life of luxury and privilege that she had fantasized about throughout the early part of the novel – and which, in a fairy-tale plot, is revealed to be her rightful inheritance – and opts instead for the more familiar life, returning to her adopted father and to Felix Holt, and the social style to which she has become accustomed. Throughout, the novel proposes that knowledge is gained from experience, and acts that have been proved to be good should be repeated. Esther demonstrates this in a small way when she self-consciously repeats actions towards her father that she has learned will please him. By contrast, Harold's marriage to a slave repeats nothing and is unrepeatable – it shatters the narrative by its uniqueness. This insistence on precedents also lies at the heart of the political message of the novel: to give the vote to a class of men who have no previous experience of voting would be a disaster, for these men would merely reproduce, at a national level, the barbarous tendencies of their present existence.[19] Better educate the working class, teach working men the responsibilities of democracy and the pitfalls of violent change. Felix Holt is a 'radical' of a strikingly conservative kind, advocating change only under carefully controlled conditions.

*Felix Holt* is the most political of Eliot's novels in the sense that it deals centrally with issues of political representation and labour disputes. But, as we have seen, it also considers questions of a more personal kind, to do with the family. The novel, however, does not really recognize a distinction between the political, public world and the private lives of individuals; as the narrator tells us early on, 'there is no private life which has not been determined by a wider public life' (*FH* 50). But, just as private lives are indeed shown to be determined by the wider public life in the course of the novel, so too private lives are somehow representative of broader political concerns. The mixed-race child, then, is more than an embellishment of Harold's exotic past. He comes to represent the unthinkable future, the idea without precedent, that punctures the surface of the narrative – the idea of radical change that cannot be countenanced within Eliot's social world. In the end, the novel advocates once again the institution of the family as the social basis for the controlled mixing of breeds, and, by implication, the implementation of gradual and constrained social change.

As we have seen, then, Eliot's novels use the idea of the family as a means of encoding messages of a social and political kind. These messages are most overt in *Felix Holt*, but they are also to be found in *Romola* and the other novels that we have looked at in this chapter. Above all, the family provides the basis for a historical model which sanctions gradual social change and the maintenance of tradition, and a belief in the slow but inexorable path of progress. In using the family in this way, Eliot was in line with many of her contemporaries who also recognized the ideological uses of the family model. What is most interesting about Eliot is the complex way in which the family interweaves ideas taken from a variety of different arenas – from philosophy, biology, and racial theory. In this chapter we have unpicked some of these strands. Clearly when Eliot writes about the family she draws on much more than her own personal experience of families.

The domestic family is central to Eliot's works in most of her great novels. However, in a number of late works, the family begins to take a different shape. Indeed, around the time that she wrote *Felix Holt*, she had begun to be interested in an idea of a family based on racial identification, rather than on ideas of domesticity – the family as a species rather than a social grouping. This new version of the family is explored most extensively in *Daniel Deronda*, but it is also the subject of Eliot's long narrative poem, *The Spanish Gypsy*, the writing of which flanked *Felix Holt*.[20] In this work, the eponymous heroine, Fedalma, relinquishes her fiancé, Don Silva, a nobleman, on the revelation of her true identify as a gypsy princess. Sacrificing personal love and domestic happiness for social duty, Fedalma realizes that she must accede to her newly discovered father's dying wish that she carry on his role as leader of the gypsies, establishing, as in *Romola*, a matriarchal society. Unlike Romola, however, Fedalma must choose between domestic happiness and social duty – between the domestic family and the 'family' of the race of gypsies. In *Romola*, by contrast, the family is first and foremost a domestic group made up of children and a mother figure, despite its profoundly symbolic function as the foundation of a new and improved society. As Dinah and Adam's family in *Adam Bede*, or Silas's family at the end of *Silas Marner*, or even Will and Dorothea's family at the end of *Middlemarch*, the family is a domestic group that doubles as a model for the larger society. In *The Spanish Gypsy*, however, the family invoked is the larger 'family' of the gypsies, and specifically not the private, domestic family. Likewise, in *Daniel Deronda*, when Daniel and Mirah travel to 'the East', they do so to establish the new 'family' of the Jewish nation state. In these two works the family's political function supersedes and effaces its domestic one. It is not that there *is* a 'private life that has not been determined by a wider public life' (*FH* 50); rather the whole notion of a private life and its relation to the public has been reconceived.

*The Spanish Gypsy* and *Daniel Deronda* share an interest in racial identity that marks a departure in Eliot's thinking about race. While elsewhere, as we have seen, her interest focuses on amalgamated or fused races, in these works she begins to consider 'pure' races – even the 'lesser race' of the gypsy – in a more positive light. Moreover, in these works, the mark of racial identity comes to be the most significant determining factor in individual lives, the effects of which, like those of Oedipus' wound, cannot be escaped. This new focus on racial identity has a profound effect on the very structure of Eliot's works. As we saw in the previous chapter, the world she presents in the earlier works tends to be one which is governed by social and economic factors, in which the material details of everyday life provide keys to the understanding of individual motivation and behaviour. In *Daniel Deronda*, as in *The Spanish Gypsy*, the determining fact of race inserts a term that is not open to such analysis. This new focus on racial identity is one of the factors that gives *Daniel Deronda* a very different feel from other works. In the next chapter we will concentrate on this novel, and explore the ways in which the realist model that Eliot had perfected in previous works is put under strain.

# 3

# The Shadow of the Coming Age: Modernity and the Limits of Realism

Until now we have concentrated our attention on Eliot's works of realist fiction. While it is true that Eliot's major achievements are within that genre – indeed, she provides us with the most accomplished examples of the realist novel in the English language – she also wrote a number of works of fiction that do not fall easily into the category. These include her supernatural novella, 'The Lifted Veil' (1859), and her last work, *The Impressions of Theophrastus Such* (1879). We should add to this group, too, her late novel, *Daniel Deronda* (1876), a work whose formal complexities have been considered by some as flaws or mistakes within its construction. In recent years, these formally eccentric or aberrant works have attracted a good deal of critical attention which, especially in the case of 'The Lifted Veil', has lifted them from relative obscurity.[1]

In this chapter we will focus on the most substantial of these works, *Daniel Deronda*, and consider it in the context of these other supposedly eccentric works. Such a grouping makes sense because, as we shall see, in all of these works Eliot explores themes and issues that could not easily be presented within the interpretative model of realism. The world conjured by these works is much more uncertain and volatile than that of the previous novels, and is inhabited by different kinds of people: those who can see into the future, like Latimer in 'The Lifted Veil'; or those whose destiny is prescribed not by social experience but by racial inheritance, even when that inheritance is unknown, as is the case for Daniel Deronda; or the shadowy acquaintances of Theophrastus Such, the inhabitants of 'crowded London drawing room[s]', whose divergent 'varieties of history' have no more substance than Theophrastus cares to imagine (*TS* 20). In the other works, material circumstances and benign human agency conspired to harness the forces of change for social progress, but in these works, as we shall see, people are subject to influences that are beyond their control and which divert the steady path of improvement.

As in previous chapters, we will contextualize *Daniel Deronda* by considering it in the light of some of the areas of contemporary debate on which Eliot drew in its composition. The first of these comes from the political arena. Eliot used *Daniel Deronda* as a vehicle for exploring questions concerning nationalism and race, which, by the 1870s when the novel was written, had attained widespread political importance. The other context that we will explore is that presented by the so-called fringe sciences, such as phrenology, mesmerism, and spiritualism. Throughout her life Eliot sustained a strong and not always sceptical interest in these fields of enquiry, but only in 'The Lifted Veil' did she use them as a basis of her fiction. While *Daniel Deronda* does not engage with this kind of material in a direct fashion, there are significant ways in which the forms of consciousness that she describes in this novel are informed by insights of similar forms of intellectual enquiry.

Both of these areas – race and the fringe sciences – inform the novel and provide us with a framework in which to understand the ways in which it diverges significantly from the novels that we discussed in the previous chapters. *Daniel Deronda* presents a different conception of the human subject, a different apprehension of historical process, and a different understanding of the world. It describes a society and a culture transformed by the processes of modernization that shaped the world at the end of the nineteenth century – the impact of new technologies, new scientific knowledge, new forms of political organization. The modernized world of this novel is one that is no longer amenable to the forms of realist fiction that Eliot had perfected in her earlier works. In this chapter, I will suggest that *Daniel Deronda* is best understood, not as an imperfect imitation of the successes of *Middlemarch*, but as a mature work which challenges the certainties of the realist form.

In the previous chapter, I discussed the priority that Eliot continually gives in her novels to private life and the family; this emphasis, I argued, is one of the characteristics of her realism. *Daniel Deronda* also focuses on the family: the Malinger and the Harleth families and their various relatives and associates provide both the characters and the context for the drama. At one level *Daniel Deronda* is a domestic drama – a tragic romance in which the beautiful but headstrong Gwendolen Harleth chooses the wrong man for the wrong reasons, and realizes the worth and attractions of the right man, Daniel Deronda, when it is too late. However, the presentation of the family in this novel is complicated by the inclusion of issues that impinge on the private, domestic lives of families. Most prominent among these is the revelation that Daniel is a Jew. With the knowledge of his true identity, he is also ascribed a destiny that will force him to leave the nurturing bosom of his adopted family, to marry Mirah, the Jewess he has saved from suicide, rather than Gwendolen, the beautiful widow. At the end of the novel, he will leave England to establish a Jewish nation state in 'the East'. By this point, Eliot has abandoned the constraints of domestic realism completely to spin instead an allegorical tale of political rejuvenation.

Unlike the other novels, *Daniel Deronda* has a forthright and radical polemical message, stronger and more apparent than in any of Eliot's other works. It is set in the context of deeply rooted English anti-Semitism, of which Lady Malinger's wish that Mirah will be converted to Christianity represents the most benign expression.[2] Throughout Eliot insists on the humanity and dignity of the Jew, correcting pejorative stereotypes that abounded at the time. As commentators have pointed out, the ending of *Daniel Deronda* gave imaginative credibility to a movement emerging at this time to establish a Jewish homeland; indeed, since its first publication the novel has served as an important foundational work for many Jews.[3] But beyond this sectarian interest, Judaism is also presented as a universal religion, the restoration of which is crucial to the revival of English culture, represented as at this moment floundering under the cultural impoverishment of finance capitalism. Reversing its usual associations with usury, Eliot offers Judaism as the regenerative agent of English national culture.

This shift into a polemical realm – what we might see as a

realm of political fantasy – diverts her from the concrete certainties of the social world that provide the usual foundation of her fiction. While the former novels had been concerned to document the details of a solid, material, and (except for *Romola*) *English*, reality, in *Daniel Deronda* the social world is made strange or exotic by the self-conscious interweaving of myths and fairy-tale plots. For instance, the Meyrick girls name Daniel 'Prince Camaralzaman' – a heroic character from the *Arabian Nights*. Although a fanciful and romantic nickname on the part of the sisters, the name directs him to a particular dramatic trajectory, as he proceeds throughout the novel to rescue women, and finally to marry Mirah, who, very early on, is referred to as Queen Budoor, Camaralzaman's wife in the tale. More striking are the allusions to religious myth in the novel. Daniel, like Christ (in fact his 'real' name is revealed to be Charisi), is the redemptive Jew, saviour of men and women. In this rendering, Gwendolen assumes the role of Mary Magdalene, the fallen woman, saved through her love of Daniel/Christ. While all of Eliot's works draw on a rich fund of classical myths, and traditional and religious stories, only in *Daniel Deronda* does the use of such elements bestow such a sense of estrangement, marking a distinct departure from her commitment to social realism. In this novel we enter a world in which events are no longer firmly rooted in material realities but rather in a more shadowy world of myths, customs, and memories.

There are other important departures too. Unlike the former novels, in which the various strands of the plot are knitted together with deliberate skill and delicacy, *Daniel Deronda* is a novel whose two major plots – Gwendolen's and Daniel's – are only uneasily attached. Despite Eliot's own stated intention that all parts of the novel should connect with each other, critics have felt the novel to be disjointed and unbalanced, lacking the formal perfection of *Middlemarch*. F. R. Leavis gave voice to many readers' feelings when he notoriously claimed that the novel should be cut up, and the Jewish strand excised, leaving only Gwendolen's story.[4] While Leavis's impatience with the Jewish story might be seen to betray a certain kind of anti-Semitism, it nevertheless points to the fact that the novel as a whole fails adequately to integrate its two halves, making it in formal terms a more complex and difficult novel than the earlier ones.

Moreover, if the earlier novels on the whole diverge only minimally from a fundamentally linear time scheme, *Daniel Deronda* begins, strikingly, in the middle of events, cuts backwards and forwards in time, and presents a much more complicated apprehension of the relationship between time and narrative. For instance, the novel opens *in medias res*, as Daniel observes Gwendolen at the gambling tables in Leubronn; in chapter 3 we return to a much earlier point in the story to hear about the events that have led up to the gambling scene, and only in chapter 21 do we resume the narrative as it was left hanging at the end of chapter 2. Throughout the novel the histories of particular characters – Daniel, Mirah, Mordecai, for instance -- are interwoven with contemporary events of the narrative, giving a complex sense of time in which every moment is seen to be thick with the traces of the past, rather than mere stages in an ever-onward progression.

All these points – the overt political project, the use of myth, the complicated temporal scheme, and uneven plot structure – conspire to make *Daniel Deronda* a different kind of novel from the works we have looked at so far. Other significant factors are its free geographical range, and the difficult relationships with their location that characters are shown to assume. Whereas in the earlier novels the majority of the significant action is located firmly in one location (usually a provincial town such as Middlemarch, Treby Magna, or St Oggs), the characters in *Daniel Deronda* roam between towns and countries and continents, shiftless and exiled, like the Jewish race which provides the thematic focus to the novel. While the earlier novels presumed that individual characters could be explained in terms of their position within a fairly closed social world, in *Daniel Deronda* there is no identification between people and places; on the contrary, characters are continually displaced. Mirah, uprooted by her wicked father, travels between Europe and America; Deronda, who throughout most of the novel mistakenly presumes himself to be the illegitimate son of his 'uncle', Sir Hugo Malinger, grows up with a profound sense of alienation from his home; and Gwendolen, bored and fractious, is repeatedly described as a 'princess in exile'. 'Pity', the narrator regrets, 'that Offendene [the house to which Gwendolen returns after the episode in Leubronn] was not the home of

Miss Harleth's childhood, or endeared to her by childhood memories! A human life, I think, should be well rooted in some spot of native land' (*DD* 50). The ending of the novel is an attempt to correct these various experiences of alienation, and 'root' people in their 'native land[s]'. Deronda draws on this metaphor in his vague wish for Gwendolen at the end that she will 'find [her] life growing like a plant' (*DD* 839) and, more broadly, in his effort to establish a Jewish homeland in which to root his own people. But the extent to which these aims are successful remains in question. The final project, to root the Jewish people in its own nation state, is speculative and inconclusive, partly because the place itself – the East – is only gestured towards in a shadowy and uncertain way. In the end, the novel remains beset by the problem of what constitutes a 'native land' in a context in which, as we are constantly aware, imperial expansion and the formation of nationalist movements render the ownership of territory a highly political issue.

All in all, the world of *Daniel Deronda* is very different from that of the earlier novels – a much bigger, busier, more uncertain and complicated world. People travel more, and more quickly, on the new modes of transportation – trains and steam ships: Grandcourt, for instance, goes overnight by train to see his former mistress, Mrs Glasher, in her house in the coal-mining district; Gwendolen travels home alone from Leubronn, 'deposited as a *feme sole*... at one of those stations which have been fixed on not as near anywhere but as equidistant from everywhere' (*DD* 269). Much of the action takes place in cities, where people of different nationalities and different races and classes mingle indiscriminately. Crowds form to watch any passing spectacle, such as the group that gathered to watch the return of the shipwrecked boat on the beach in Genoa, or 'the usual groups' that gathered 'to see the departing company' (*DD* 804) as Mirah leaves a society concert one morning in London. In both cases, the crowds of strangers also contain intimates – Deronda is in the crowd watching Gwendolen land on the beach, while Mirah's own father mingles in the London crowd. The crowd homogenizes everyone, regardless of identity or purpose, and renders everyone a stranger. Much emphasis is laid on the mixed nationalities and racial types in the crowd: on the beach Deronda listens to the 'clamorous talk in various languages' (*DD* 749), and in another crowd, that gathered in the gambling hall in Leubronn, there are 'Livonian and Spanish, Graeco-Italian and miscellaneous German, English aristocratic and English plebian' (*DD* 36).

The word 'crowd' is used very frequently in this novel, but generally in a figurative sense, indicating a loss of an individual's will or agency. Hence Mirah warns Mordecai that Deronda's life may be 'like a crowd in which he had got entangled' (*DD* 721). Most often the crowd is used to describe mental states of intensity and confusion: Rex has 'a tumultuary crowd of thoughts' (*DD* 776) and Gwendolen's 'crowding reflections . . . quell[ing] her resistance' to Grandcourt (*DD* 659); later her 'indignation . . . was getting merged in a crowd of other feelings, dim and alarming as a crowd of ghosts' (*DD* 662); and Mirah 'was pressed upon by a crowd of thoughts thrusting themselves forward as interpreters on that consciousness which still remained unuttered to herself' (*DD* 796). In all these examples the crowd tends to have a ghostly or dreamlike quality, ushering in new states of consciousness that are peculiarly disturbing. In the crowd of reflections, as in a crowd of people, the recognizable self is lost, and characters are estranged even from themselves.

The continual awareness of the crowd is a significant characteristic of *Daniel Deronda*. While crowd scenes occur in Eliot's previous novels – for instance, the crowd of striking men in *Felix Holt*, or the hecklers at Mr Brooke's speech at the hustings in *Middlemarch* – these crowds have a different constituency and purpose to the shifting and shiftless crowds of the later novel.[5] In the earlier works, crowds tend to be made up of a single type of people – usually the anonymous working class – and the scenes in which they appear constitute the rare moments in which they have an opportunity to express their grievances, albeit in this inarticulate and violent way. But, as we have seen, the crowd in *Daniel Deronda* has no such unity, nor such singleness of purpose. The promiscuous and seemingly formless commingling of people in *Daniel Deronda* links to a new idea of a mass society that emerged in the second half of the century and which was repeatedly represented through the idea of the crowd. From mid-century onwards, in political and sociological writings, as well as in literary works, the idea of the crowd came to encapsulate a new and distinctly modern, urban kind of experience: at once thrilling and dangerous, alienating and liberating, it tended to be associated with change, and be the harbinger of the new.[6] *Daniel Deronda* presents a society that has many of the characteristics of this modern society: a society made up of consumers rather than producers (unlike previous novels, virtually no one makes anything in *Daniel Deronda*, although plenty of objects are bought and sold); in which wealth is made (and lost) through speculation rather than through industry and labour (not just in the casino at Leubronn – Gwendolen's family loses all its money on the stock exchange when 'Grapnell and Co. [fail] for a million' (*DD* 43) ); a world of advertising and commercialism, in which even families may be discovered through advertisement (for instance, Daniel considers advertising for Mirah's lost family), and individual talents must be marketed to a consuming public (as in the case of Mirah); a world in which traditional certainties have been eroded in the constant traffic of capital and information. All this marks out *Daniel Deronda* as a novel that squarely considers the condition of modernity in the context of a society that has already been transformed by new technologies.

Alert to these factors, many commentators have assumed that, unlike the other novels which are located in the past, *Daniel Deronda* is set in Eliot's contemporary time. This, however, is not the case, for it, too, is located historically, albeit in a more recent period. *Daniel Deronda* is set very deliberately in 1865 – some ten years before Eliot began to work on it. As usual, the precise historical context is of great significance – in this case, not specifically for any local or even national event, but rather for those that take place on the world stage: the American civil war, the slave uprising in Jamaica, the activities of Bismarck in Europe, the unification of Italy. The preoccupations of the time that crowd the backdrop of this novel are the activities of nationalist movements across Europe, the formation of new nation states – Germany and Italy, for instance – and the struggles for independence of oppressed peoples – in particular Negroes and, of course, Jews. Such concerns are constantly referred to throughout the text, not only in conversations between characters, or in allusions in the narrative, but also in the themes of the novel. Deronda's plans to establish a Jewish nation state are clearly in accord with the spirit of nationalism that infuses the book. But the grand emancipatory struggles of races and nations are also presented as a paradigm for explaining smaller, more domestic struggles. We are encouraged to see Gwendolen's marriage to the cruel and domineering Grandcourt as a bondage that is similar to that of a slave; in this respect, the detail that the Harleth family fortune originally was made on Caribbean plantations assumes telling significance. Moreover, the various illegitimate children who occupy much of the novel (Grandcourt's children by Mrs Glasher, and Deronda – although, of course, he is latterly revealed to be of legitimate birth) have a position that parallels that of particular racial groups who are also oppressed by the mere circumstances of their birth.

This preoccupation with the determining effects of race and nation lies behind the most significant difference between *Daniel Deronda* and Eliot's other novels. The earlier works, as we have already seen, are built on the assumption that individuals and events are open to *social* explanations. Characters tend to be represented as the products of their material circumstances within society – hence the emphasis on mundane but telling details that we identified in Chapter 1. Conversely, all acts are considered to have direct social impacts, and the best acts are the sympathetic ones, carried out in the interests of others. In *Middlemarch* Eliot develops these tenets most extensively by introducing the metaphor of the doctor's diagnostic gaze. Here events and characters are scrutinized as though they are the symptoms of a social body: ultimately they are open not only to analysis and understanding, but also to cure. In *Daniel Deronda,* however, we are constantly aware of an impulse at work that remains beyond this understanding gaze, a force that is not reducible to social explanations. There is evidence of a deeper and more visceral impulse at work directing the course of events – the determination of race. Thus Deronda's fate is sealed with the revelation of his racial identity. His inheritance is implanted in his blood, and transcends – even denies – the forces of upbringing and society.

Deronda's search for his true familial origins – his biological roots – is thus crucial to this novel. In many ways this is a traditional theme of the genre of the novel and has been explored elsewhere in Eliot's work. *Silas Marner*, *Felix Holt*, and, to a lesser extent, *Middlemarch* all have plots which involve the revelation of the parentage of key characters. But, whereas in *Silas Marner* and *Felix Holt* Eppie and Esther both reject the claims of their natural parents, opting instead for the moral superiority but material poverty of their adoptive families, Daniel Deronda enthusiastically embraces the inheritance of his biological family. Indeed, the message of *Silas Marner* and *Felix Holt* is that it is not only possible, but *right*, to break the lines of family inheritance. In both these cases, the families that attempt to restore their lost inheritors are decadent and in decline – morally and biologically too (in *Silas Marner* Godfrey Cass and his wife are unable to have children, and in *Felix Holt* the Transome family is not only financially broke, but deteriorating mentally and physically). In *Middlemarch*, under different circumstances, Ladislaw also rejects an inheritance – money owed to his mother by Bulstrode. Here, inherited money is tainted money, stained with the moral corruption of the past. (Significantly, the money came from Ladislaw's Jewish, money-lending grandfather. The sustained and purposefully sympathetic treatment of Jews in *Daniel Deronda* is a new theme for Eliot.) In these novels, then, characters make moral choices that diverge from the social circumstances of their birth, when that is understood primarily in terms of their family's position and material wealth. In *Daniel Deronda*, on the contrary, the revealed inheritance is specifically *not* material wealth or social position, but a rich and extensive cultural history – contained in a box of documents that Daniel eventually retrieves from Frankfurt – and a racial identity that is inscribed on the very body of the man.[7] The possibility that he might choose to forgo his inheritance, in the way that Eppie, or Esther, or Ladislaw does, is diminished by the fact that his inheritance is manifest in his physical being.

Throughout the novel Deronda cannot escape the particularities of his appearance, his darkness, and, in particular, his deep and penetrating gaze – the gaze of the Jew. Incredibly, he is recognized by his grandfather's friend, Kalonymos, when, by chance, he visits a synagogue in Frankfurt; although Daniel has no social links with the synagogue, nor even has any knowledge of his own ancestry, Kalonymos is struck by the resemblance of Daniel's features to his grandfather's. While Esther, in *Felix Holt*, displays vestiges of her ancestry in her refined bearing and polite manners, this is an inheritance that shapes her destiny in no profound way. But Daniel's ancestry is branded in the racially distinct marks of his body, and it determines the future of his life. This emphasis on racial determination diminishes the extent to which an individual can be considered to be the author of his or her own destiny, and the degree to which he or she is shaped by the social environment. Characters such as Esther and Eppie are shown to be formed in the society in which they lived, educated through experience, so that they are able to make reasoned choices about their futures. But Daniel's destiny predates his social experience: it becomes a matter of revelation rather than education.

The idea that one's life could be determined by factors other than social ones – for example, racial inheritance – was one that fascinated Eliot throughout her life, even though in other works she did not explore their impact to the extent that she does in *Daniel Deronda*. As we noted in the previous chapter, in earlier works she began to examine the racial theories that were in circulation at the time. But, in *Daniel Deronda*, the preoccupation with Daniel's race absorbs much of the novel. It is important to remember that these racial theories had intellectual roots in a much wider network of interests in the fringe sciences, including phrenology, mesmerism, and spiritualism, which all in different ways regarded the body as an instinctual and irrational entity. Eliot's fascination with the fringe sciences dates back to her early twenties. Through her friendship with Charles Bray, she became interested first in phrenology and then related sciences, and began to mix with a circle of intellectuals working in these fields, including the phrenologist George Combe, Harriet Martineau, whose extensive interest in the fringe sciences was notorious, and William Ballantyne Hodgson, amateur phrenologist and Principal of the Liverpool Mechanics Institute, who, at a party in 1844, mesmerized Eliot for fun.[8] Such interests were sustained throughout her life: Haight records another vignette much later – Eliot's visit to a spiritualist seance, in 1874 (during the period in which she was working on *Daniel Deronda*), held at the house of relatives of Charles Darwin. The Darwins, along with various other scientists and intellectuals of their acquaintance, were present. The assembled company was relieved when Eliot and Lewes left early, for Lewes had interrupted the proceedings, according to one the participants, by being 'troublesome and inclined to make jokes and not play the game fairly and sit in the dark in silence' (*GEB* 469). Despite this manifest impatience, Eliot and Lewes were no less fascinated by (but possibly more sceptical of) occurrences of paranormal phenomena than others who moved in their liberal intellectual circles. For many, including Eliot and Lewes, irrational states such as mesmeric trances, somnambulance, or clairvoyance – states in which the body's instincts took over from reason – offered valuable evidence in the pursuit of a fuller understanding of the human mind.

Explanations of human behaviour based on these kinds of experiences have little scientific credibility today, but, in Eliot's day, not only were they taken seriously by some intellectuals as promising branches of science, but, moreover, they were very important in the development of fields of enquiry that have had lasting impact. For instance, the investigations of paranormal states such as mesmerism or somnambulance played an important role in the development of the psychoanalytic theories that took shape at the end of the century.[9] Phrenology, the science which held that the bumps on the head presented an index of the power of the various functions of the brain, exerted extensive influence throughout the century, and provided a basis for subsequent developments in a broad range of disciplines, such as psychology, anthropology, and education, as well as in various social theories.[10] Significantly, it also provided a scientific basis for the new biologically based racial theories, suggesting that particular characteristics and facilities of human intelligence could be directly linked to specific racial groups through studying their characteristic physiological forms.[11] Eliot had a particular interest in phrenology, and in 1844 went so far as to have a cast made of her head, which revealed to George Combe that 'in the brain-development, the Intellect greatly predominates.... In the Feelings, the Animal and Moral regions are about equal; the Moral being quite sufficient to keep the animal in order and in due subservience...The social feelings [are] very active...She [is] of a most affectionate disposition' (*GEB* 51) – a reading that has had an uncanny influence on even twentieth-century biographies.[12]

In the context of Eliot's lively interest in the fringe sciences it is perhaps surprising that, before *Daniel Deronda*, she had paid relatively little attention to them in her fiction. The work in which they receive the fullest treatment is her novella, 'The Lifted Veil' – a story which even Eliot considered to be *outré*.[13] 'The Lifted Veil' is a macabre tale about a clairvoyant, Latimer, whose terrible fate is revealed to him during mesmeric trances. Despite having foreseen the fatal consequences of marrying the cold, fortune-seeking beauty, Bertha, he nevertheless fails to act on this knowledge, until the final revelation that Bertha intends to poison him. This revelation is gained through the unorthodox experimentation of his doctor friend, who, through a blood transfusion, brings back from the dead Bertha's maid, the accomplice in the crime. At the time of publication, the revivification of the maid was certainly the most controversial aspect of the story, for it raised the spectre of Dr Frankenstein, another transgressive scientist, who had offended against moral injunctions as much as he had against scientific orthodoxy. Indeed, in every way, the centrality of para-scientific explanations gave this work a very different feel in comparison with Eliot's other works. While elsewhere, as we have seen, events were firmly rooted in social and moral explanations, in 'The Lifted Veil', as in *Daniel Deronda*, different patterns of causality seem to be in play, which, in this case, stretch the imagination beyond the limits of usual experience and moral orthodoxy. For Eliot, then, scientific enquiry seems to put a strain on the explanatory model that usually shapes her fiction. In fact, this is even more exaggeratedly the case in 'The Lifted Veil' than in *Daniel Deronda*: in the former she conspicuously abandons the measured tone of social realism for the excesses of sensation fiction, a genre made popular by writers such as Wilkie Collins or Mary Braddon.[14]

'The Lifted Veil' and *Daniel Deronda* both exhibit a preference for scientific explanations. For instance, in both works, phrenology provides a key to understanding human character and behaviour. Latimer's feeble character is explained by a phrenologist who locates his deficiency, not in terms of education or influence, but on 'the upper sides of his head' (*L.* v. 6), and in *Daniel Deronda*, when Kalonymos remarks on Daniel's resemblance to his grandfather, he notes that Charisi had 'one deep upright line in his brow' (*DD* 790) denoting his 'iron will' – an uncompromising sternness, the signs of which are lacking in the softer-faced, and softer-mannered, Daniel. Moreover, in 'The Lifted Veil' the plot is structured around moments at which bodies provide pieces of knowledge that are otherwise unavailable to the characters and at odds with social experience, first in the form of Latimer's mesmerized trances, and second through the revivification of the maid. In *Daniel Deronda*, it is Daniel's racial inheritance – which is also described as a kind of *instinct* – that determines his proper destiny.

This shared emphasis on an instinctual body which behaves in irrational and impulsive ways suggests that 'The Lifted Veil' could be seen as the precursor to *Daniel Deronda*. It sets both apart from Eliot's other works in which characters are subject to patterns of motivation that are more visible and open to rational explanations. In these works, however, characters are driven by impulses that are unseen and somehow mysterious. Daniel, for instance, is subject to his 'impetuous determining impulse' which provokes him to retrieve Gwendolen's necklace and to save Mirah from drowning, and Gwendolen is repeatedly described as responding 'automatically': she 'automatically looked in the glass' (*DD* 62); she 'bow[ed] herself out' from Mirah's 'automatically' (*DD* 651). When offered her burnous by Lush, she 'simply follow[ed] antipathy and inclination' in refusing it (*DD* 159), without consideration of the consequences of her act. Gwendolen's gambling also indicates a disturbing willingness to relinquish her will or agency to what Eliot describes in chapter 1 as 'automatic' forces: the call to lay bets in the gambling hall is 'the automatic voice of destiny' (*DD* 39), and the noise of gambling is compared to that issuing from 'an ingeniously constructed automaton' (*DD* 35). This mechanical aspect of human behaviour corresponds with the social and historical setting for the novel: in this newly automated world, people, too, are transformed into machines, losing their powers of self-determination to the greater will of technology.

In its linking of the instinctual body and industrial processes, *Daniel Deronda* shares something with *Silas Marner*: as I suggested in the previous chapter, in the course of the latter novel, Silas's mechanical being is somehow made organic, as the alienated industrial worker is incorporated into the rural, organic community. The plot of *Daniel Deronda* has a similar trajectory. Here, too, there is an insistent strand of the narrative that wishes to see the instinctual or mechanical bodies of individuals, such as Gwendolen or Daniel, and of societies, transformed into organic ones. In this respect, Daniel's attempt to set up a Jewish nation state at the end of the novel is seen as the establishment of an organic society in contrast to the alienated, mechanical society of modern England. But, in *Daniel Deronda,* the two ideas of the instinctual and the organic are much more complex and nuanced than in the earlier work. Indeed, the emergence of the organic body is a much more complicated enterprise, and in fact is never fully achieved: for instance, while Daniel expresses the wish that Gwendolen's life should 'grow like a plant', she continues to be subject to the automatic responses that plague her throughout, and, as we have noted, the Jewish nation state is not in fact achieved within the confines of the narrative. While in the earlier novels the organic society is associated with a pre-existing historical moment and is represented as a reversion to an earlier state, in *Daniel Deronda* the organic society will be the result of a future historical change that is only alluded to in the novel.

The new complexities of these terms in *Daniel Deronda* reflect Eliot's later thinking about a nexus of ideas concerning psychology, memory, and culture, which was informed by scientific thinking of the time. By the 1870s scientific interest in these more shadowy realms had become intense, and, in its probing of such issues, *Daniel Deronda* is very much a novel of its time. Significantly, during the period in which Eliot was working on it, George Henry Lewes began to write his great psychological treatise, *Problems of Life and Mind.* Lewes's work provides a useful scientific context in which to understand aspects of Eliot's novel; the two works inform each other, and seem to engage in a dialogue.

Lewes's *Problems of Life and Mind* is an extension – on a large scale – of the organic theories that I discussed in Chapter 2. His aim was to produce a theory of the mind that would draw together philosophy and science, and steer a course between the two explanatory models that had dominated the century – idealism and materialism: between a theory which considers life and mind to be the products of a metaphysical principle, and one which considers them to be constituted of organisms that are explicable in the rational terms of mechanical laws.[15] As a scientist himself, Lewes admits that he is inclined to agree with the materialists that, in their individual operations, organisms do indeed function as mechanisms. But, he observes, there are various properties that are integral to organic forms that cannot be explained in terms of mechanical laws. First, he argues, organisms have a capacity for feeling or sentiment. Moreover, this capacity for feeling makes it possible for organic forms to learn from experience and to change. Thus, he asserts, organic forms have a historical dimension, which is manifest not only in the slow evolutionary changes of species, but also in the growth and development of individual beings. He sees this impulse for change, not as a mechanical principle, but as a manifestation of consciousness or the will. The processes of development and growth – or, as Lewes would say, of history – are attributed to consciousness rather than instinct.

Thus far Lewes is in accord with the early Eliot, whose works, as we have seen, depicted the growth of human individuals (for instance, Silas Marner, Esther, or Dorothea) and societies (Raveloe or Middlemarch) in terms of the development or refinement of consciousness. However, Lewes describes this process of growth in more detail as specifically the *repression* of the instincts through consciousness. The ontogenic development characteristic of human subjects, he argues, is one in which the original instinctual responses of the body are gradually controlled through the imposition of consciousness or the will. Thus the process of growth or civilization is seen as one in which the body emerges from an instinctual, and thus mechanical, state to one that, according to Lewes, is increasingly *organic*. In moments of passion or excitement, the subject may relapse into an older condition of instinctual response (or, indeed, under hypnotism or in some other special psychic conditions), but, Lewes insists, once inscribed on the mind, the fundamental force of consciousness is indelible. In its emphasis on the repression of the instincts, Lewes's theory is a precursor of Freud's psychoanalytic theory.[16] But Lewes's work has an altogether more optimistic cast to it, focusing less on the return of repressed material than on the triumph of consciousness in the mastery of the instincts. For Lewes, the organic state in which the subject's or society's being has been mastered by consciousness is the mature, developed, and conscious state to which all aspire.

The two components of Lewes's psychological theory that stand out are, first, the insistence on the reflective aspects of consciousness that is necessary for organic growth; and, second, the emphasis on the repressive function of consciousness. Both these points interestingly inform the development of characters in *Daniel Deronda*, but they also provide Eliot with the basis for further exploration. For instance, as we have already observed, Daniel's destiny is prescribed by his racial origin – which is something like an instinct – that is revealed to him during the course of the novel. However, Eliot throughout emphasizes the cultural dimension of his racial legacy – the fact that he inherits not only a physiological identity, but a box of documents denoting a culture and an evolving history. Daniel's response to his inherited past is a reflective one: he professes to Kalonymos, 'I shall call myself a Jew... But I will not say that I shall profess to believe exactly as my fathers have believed. Our fathers themselves changed the horizon of their belief and learned of other races...', to which Kalonymos replies, 'You are Daniel Charisi's grandson' (*DD* 792). Daniel's development should be seen in Lewes's terms as specifically an *organic* one: his history and culture allow him consciously to reflect on, embrace, and transform or modify his racial past. At this point, Daniel's individual growth and that of the Jewish race coincide; this drawing-together of ontogenic and phylogenic aspects allows Daniel to stand metonymically for the whole race – and the new Jewish nation. By making this identification between race and nation, Eliot applies Lewes's notion of organic development to the idea of the nation – a step that Lewes himself did not take. Indeed, Lewes claimed that 'there is no national consciousness that is equivalent to the individual consciousness, because there is no national unity that is equivalent to the individual unity'.[17] But, in *Daniel Deronda*, the establishment of a Jewish nation state provides Eliot with a model in which national consciousness *can* aspire to equivalence with individual consciousness, through the idea of a cultural memory mediated by racial identification: the nation in an organic condition – truly unified through the reflections of a common consciousness.

Daniel's individual organic self emerges through his conscious reflections on his racial or instinctual legacy. But, as we have already observed, this emergent consciousness necessitates the repression of other instinctive impulses: his sympathetic impulse to save people in trouble or distress – for example, Gwendolen, Mirah, and Hans. '[L]ove and duty had thrown other bonds around him,' we are told, 'and that impulse could no longer determine his life' (*DD* 834). In the course of the novel, Daniel evolves from an impulsively kind, yet rootless, young man, to the mature and reflective Jew, possessing a strong sense of cultural and religious duty. In this respect, Eliot follows the trajectory of organic development that Lewes outlined in his psychological work. However, in contrast to Lewes, Eliot seems transfixed by the failures of the repressive process, as the narrative keeps returning to points at which Daniel's residual, instinctive self re-emerges. In his final meeting alone with Gwendolen, Daniel's old 'impulse' came back as a 'painful quivering'. The interview is constrained and awkward: 'there was no smile between them as they met and clasped hands' (*DD* 836). Later 'Deronda automatically took up his hat', and Gwendolen 'felt her heart giving a great leap, as if it too had a consciousness of its own...' (*DD* 838). As we have already noted, the characters in *Daniel Deronda*, including Daniel, fail to become organic individuals in whom consciousness has triumphed over instinctual behaviour, in the way that Lewes describes. Despite his emergence as a conscious Jew and founder of the organic nation state, Daniel will remain the victim of his old impulsive self.

The continual return of repressed instincts in *Daniel Deronda* complicates Eliot's attempts to find the organic resolution that she seeks. Indeed, this is a complex novel because it is subject to contradictory and irresolvable pressures. On the one hand, Lewes's psychological theory provides her with a framework in which to conceptualize an idea of organic development that suits her political vision. But, on the other hand, Lewes's emphasis on repression triggers for Eliot a contrary interest in the failures of the mechanisms of repression, so that the possibility of organic development of consciousness, particularly as it pertains to the individual, will always be frustrated. Thus throughout *Daniel Deronda* there is a constant awareness of a level of experience that is somehow beyond consciousness: frequent allusions to paranormal or supernatural effects that defy understanding, or to a realm of instinctual behaviour that marks the body in seemingly irrational ways. The novel is steeped in references to the fringe sciences: Gwendolen wishes to have telepathic communication with Daniel, and elsewhere is subject to uncontrollable fits of hysteria, which, as Jacqueline Rose has pointed out, resemble the descriptions of hysteria to be found in Freud's work.[18] There are numerous references to spirits and mediums: Sir Hugo informs Gwendolen (whom he repeatedly calls a 'spirited girl') that the Abbey is haunted by the spirits of past generations which Gwendolen hopes will 'know their place and keep underground' (*DD* 461); earlier, when Gwendolen breaks down on seeing the panel of the dead head during her performance as Hermione in *The Winter's Tale*, a voice from the assembled company accounts for the appearance of the panel in terms of 'the spirits'. 'But there is no medium present,' replies another voice. To which a third responds, 'How do you know that? We must conclude that there is, when such things happen' (*DD* 92). The interchange is particularly striking because, unusually for Eliot, none of the voices is identified. Indeed, the whole scene seems to mimic the form of a seance, deviating entirely from the codes of domestic realism.

Throughout the text we are aware of the lingering presence of the spirits of past generations and, in particular, the ways in which they haunt individual characters. The particular focus in *Daniel Deronda*, however, is not so much on the activities of spirits or spiritualists, but rather specifically on the memory, as the faculty through which the past might return to individuals. Frequently it is seen to be an involuntary force, bringing back experiences and feelings in spite of the will of the individual. Daniel's memory restores to him a past that unites him with a people and provides him with a social cause, but for others it is a more unsettling force. Gwendolen, in particular, suffers the ill effects of involuntary memories. 'Things repeat themselves on me', she tells Deronda. 'They come back – they will all come back' (*DD* 840). In *Daniel Deronda*, characters are subject to the effects of this kind of memory – a force which disrupts their conscious lives, returning repressed material in awkward ways. Unlike the cultural memory that allows the unification of national consciousness, individual memory is represented in a far less positive way. Rather than a mechanism of harmonious unity, the individual memory is seen to be a disruptive, fracturing force, unsettling the surface of individual consciousness.

This is particularly evident in the case of Gwendolen, who is held in the grip of instinctual forces beyond her control. As we have already noticed, Gwendolen, like Daniel, is presented as an individual who, in Lewes's terms, must embark on the uneasy path from a mechanical or instinctual state to a potentially organic state, in which her life might 'grow like a plant'. The instinctual aspects of Gwendolen, though, are emphasized more than in any other character, and the extent to which she manages to control them throughout is left in doubt. She repeatedly assumes the appearance of a constructed and otherwise controlled being, frequently described as appearing like a statue: as, for instance, when she and Grandcourt embark on their final sailing trip, 'like creatures who were fulfilling a supernatural destiny', she 'was declared to be like a statue' (*DD* 745). Indeed the early episode in which she attempts to enact the scene from *The Winter's Tale* is particularly significant because the part she plays is that of Hermione, the statue that returns to life. As Gwendolen's performance of this scene of animation is interrupted by a hysterical outburst on her seeing the panel, the narrative casts an ironic comment on her own process of maturation to the organic state. The dead head on the panel is significant because it prefigures the dead head of Grandcourt that she glimpses as he drowns. This connection between the two scenes is telling because it underlines the point that it is not merely the case that Gwendolen must liberate herself from the domineering control of Grandcourt; she must also free herself from her own instincts, over which she has equally little control. Indeed, she frequently tells Deronda that she is afraid of herself, of what she might do. It is as though she has another, aggressive self which endangers her own self. In this sense, then, Grandcourt, for all his tyrannical nastiness, could be seen as merely a facet of her second self – the instinctual and dangerous other half, from which she is continually at threat. The death of Grandcourt represents the subduing of her instinctual self which is necessary to allow her to proceed to a fully organic state – although the extent to which she achieves this is unclear, the only evidence being a letter written to Daniel on his wedding day, in which she remembers his wish 'that [she] may live to be one of the best of women' (*DD* 882).

Throughout *Daniel Deronda*, Eliot draws on and explores the psychological framework provided by Lewes's *Problems of Life and Mind*, but she departs from his ideas on important issues, finding instead more complex versions of human mind. Another example of this is presented by Lewes's examination of the topical question of animal automatism, an area of popular scientific and philosophical study; it concerned the extent to which living beings might be conceived as instinctual organisms, motivated by the mechanisms internal to their bodies, or, alternatively, as fully conscious beings well in control of their faculties. The possibility that man might be a machine or an automaton was aired in pamphlets and lectures of the time, provoked by scientific experiments on the nervous system, and the various branches of psychical research.[19] Lewes's notion of the conscious, organic body circumvented the worrying philosophical implications of the idea of the automatic body. For him, no matter how diminished it might be, the consciousness would always be in evidence. As an example, he provides the instance of an angry man who stabs an enemy. The man is 'struck with horror at the sight of the bleeding corpse, and passionately declares he did not *mean* to kill. Nor did he will the consequences of his act, yet he certainly willed each separate step – he recognised the knife, saw the bystanders, knew they would interfere with him, willed to push them aside. He may be right in declaring that the act was involuntary, but assuredly it was not purely mechanical.'[20]

Such morally uncertain moments, when responsibility is difficult to apportion, are common in Eliot's fiction: there are frequent instances of characters whose acts committed under pressure or in passion have consequences way beyond the expectations of the agent. *Daniel Deronda* presents a particularly fraught case in the death of Grandcourt, but here the issues are even more complex. Indeed, Gwendolen presents the opposite case of a character who certainly wills the outcome of a murderous act, but, curiously, did not necessarily cause it. Her guilt remains in doubt even at the end. The question revolves around whether or not she could have saved her husband. In her muddled account, she says that she withheld the rope because she willed his death: 'my heart said "Die!" – and he sank; and I felt "It is done – I am wicked, I am lost!" – and I had the rope in my hand – I don't know what I thought – I was leaping away from myself – I would have saved him then. I was leaping from my crime, and there it was – close to me as I fell – there was the dead face . . .' (*DD* 761). Daniel considers it unlikely that she made a difference, that, 'quite apart from it, the death was inevitable' (*DD* 762), and the fishermen who witness the event believe that Gwendolen threw herself into the water to save him. Distinct from Lewes's account of the angry man, then, in this incident, not only is the will uncertain and open to change, but, moreover the relationship between acts and effects is brought seriously into question. Gwendolen veers between a situation of imagined omnipotence, in which she wishes her husband dead and he dies, and one in which her acts make no difference whatsoever – Grandcourt's death is accidental, the unlucky combination of material effects. The narrative makes no judgement as to which account is the more accurate, leaving the impression that such knowledge is, in any case, impossible to obtain.

In contrast to Lewes's account of the angry man, in which the question was of whether or not acts and their consequences are willed, *Daniel Deronda* presents the much more worrying situation in which the realm of the mind is detached from that of the material world. Here we are presented with a world in which individuals are subject to complex and conflicted psychical states, in which motives and desires can no longer be seen as coincident with material effects. This is a solipsistic world, in which private fantasy and public events have separate trajectories. It is a far cry from Eliot's earlier novels, in which she insists on the public dimension of all private affairs.

Gwendolen's disordered private world, although the experience of a deranged individual, is nevertheless presented in *Daniel Deronda* as the inevitable product of the conditions of the modern world. Alienated, displaced, dispossessed – or, as is the case here, *possessed* by dissociated memories of the past – individuals within the world of *Daniel Deronda* are destined to be unable to make an impact, never to be able to engage with the material circumstances of their environment, somehow exiled from the immediacy of the present. The idea of the organic community of the Jewish nation state is clearly interposed as the corrective to this. But even this remains at the end of the novel nothing more than an idea, a projected future in a distant land.

There is a pessimistic note at the end of *Daniel Deronda* which is absent from earlier works. The idea of an organic community remains a fairly tenuous dream, and, moreover, individual characters, such as Gwendolen, are still beset by involuntary memories, unable to achieve the state of mature rootedness that was hoped for her. In the world of this novel, people can never be at home; and, as we have noted, the strained relationship between them and their environments is reflected in the disjointed formal organization of the novel. Such discrepancies in the form of the novel are extended further in Eliot's last work, *The Impressions of Theophrastus Such*, which she wrote in 1878, shortly before Lewes's death.

In this work, Eliot invoked the persona of an elderly cleric, similar to the narrator of her first work, *Scenes of Clerical Life*. In the complexity and obscurity of its references, the wit, and wry social observation, the work bears Eliot's signature, but in all other respects it is very different. With the exception of Theophrastus, Eliot makes no attempt to make the characters 'rounded' or psychologically convincing: all are merely pegs on which to hang Theophrastus's impressions. Recalling the automata-like form assumed by the characters in *Daniel Deronda*, one reviewer noted Eliot's 'unsympathy with her own puppets'.[21] Her commitment to plot and to the exigencies of domestic realism are abandoned. Rather this is a series of short essays which record, as the title tells us, Theophrastus's impressions of the past, the present, and, most importantly, the future. As in *Daniel Deronda*, Eliot is now concerned less with the past and tradition than with the transformations of modernity. In *The Impressions of Theophrastus Such* she extends her bleak vision of the modern world and imagines a future constructed in its likeness.

The penultimate chapter, 'The Shadow of the Coming Race', is typical of the style and content of Theophrastus's impressions. This is a conversation between Theophrastus and his friend, Trost, a whole-hearted enthusiast for science and the benefits of the machine age. Whilst Trost celebrates the uses of machinery as mankind's 'slaves', Theophrastus is fearful that the machines possess the potential to usurp, first, human labour, and second, human life. Ironically, Theophrastus's dehumanized vision of the future, in which human life is superseded by machines, is in some ways more radical than Trost's version of the future; Trost imagines the future merely as a modification of life as he already knows it. For him, machines are 'simply extensions of the human organism . . . limbs immeasurably more powerful, ever more subtle finger-tips, ever more mastery over the invisibly great and the invisibly small' (*TS* 130). For Theophrastus, on the other hand, they are 'inorganic combinations, which will carry on the elaborate processes as mutely and painlessly as we are now told that the minerals are metamorphosing themselves continually in the dark laboratory of the earth's crust' (*TS* 133).

Theophrastus's vision is a fairly familiar scenario from science fiction – a genre that was enjoying some popularity at this time. In fact, the author Samuel Butler went so far as to accuse Eliot of having plagiarized his fantasy of a world taken over by machines in *Erewhon* (1872). But what distinguishes Eliot's version is the fact that Theophrastus appears to describe not exactly a world of machines, but rather one in which humans begin to be conceived of as machines: a world peopled by characters of automatic responses and machine-like behaviour – characters not unlike Gwendolen and the impulsive Daniel. The 'Coming Age' invoked here is not one in which machines usurp human life, but rather one in which humans live in disordered psychic states, subject to unconscious and uncontrollable impulses. Thus in the discussion of the two 'races', as Eliot puts it, the emphasis is on the unconscious nature of the one, and the *consciousness* of the other: 'the immensely more powerful unconscious race' (*TS* 133) which is able to displace the 'feebler race, whose corporeal adjustments happened to be accompanied with a maniacal consciousness which imagined itself moving its mover'. 'Thus', Theophrastus tells us, 'this planet may be filled with beings who will be blind and deaf as the inmost rock, yet will execute changes as delicate and complicated as those of human language and all the intricate web of what we call its effects, without sensitive impression, without sensitive impulse: there may be, let us say, mute orations, mute rhapsodies, mute discussions, and no consciousness there even to enjoy the silence' (*TS* 133). This is the disordered universe of the machine age, populated by impaired beings who act without conscious motivation and without 'sensitive impressions' – that is, without effects that could be apprehended in the material world. In the dissociation of act and effect, and the absence of motivation, these machines are like Gwendolen, the hysteric, whose acts were also wrenched from the material world, and spurred by motives that were unconscious to her. They are the antithesis of the characters of earlier works, whose conscious motives and their material effects constitute the very fabric of the texts.

In the end, Theophrastus dismisses his ideas as 'melancholy fancies. Nobody really holds them' (*TS* 134), he declares. 'They bear the same relation to real belief as walking on the head for a show does to running away from an explosion or walking fast to catch the train.' These final, confusing *non sequiturs* repeat in an exaggerated form the sense of dislocation between act and effect that we noticed in *Daniel Deronda*. The term 'real belief' suggests the traditional world of organic communities conjured up in Eliot's earlier works: the context for solid belief, as opposed to the chimeras of modern life, represented as explosions and trains. But in this passage the sentiment undercuts itself. Real belief is compared to the pointless and unproductive display of 'walking on the head'; in comparison, the world of explosions and trains is a world of material certainties and real effects. This image of modernity is troubling, not least because it is one in which Eliot ascribes herself and Theophrastus the position of a trace of a past now extinct. She writes herself out of the picture as a quaint anachronism in a changed world.

The sense of disturbance that we noticed in *Daniel Deronda* is increased in *The Impressions of Theophrastus Such*. Not only is this an uncomfortably dislocated world, but one from which the author herself finds that she has been displaced. Describing an environment marked by technological change and new conceptions of the human subject, Eliot enacts her own extinction – unable or unwilling to adapt to the circumstances of the new age. It is inevitable that this will be her last work.

George Henry Lewes died in November 1878. Eliot's reaction was extreme: the servants commented on 'the screams [that were] heard throughout the house' (*GEB* 516), and for a number of months after the death she refused virtually all social contact. In her grief, she busied herself with the manuscript of Lewes's as yet unfinished magnum opus, *The Problems of Life and Mind*, redrafting and assembling parts of the text from Lewes's copious notes. The fruits of her labour were published the following year, around the same time as *The Impressions of Theophrastus Such*.

Eliot herself outlived Lewes by only two years. Although she wrote no more fiction after Lewes's death, her final years were hardly uneventful. In May 1880 she consented to marry John Cross. Finally at the age of 60, Eliot, who had lived for over twenty years on the peripheries of society as, to all intents and purposes, a fallen woman, became a respectable wife. Her brother, Isaac, whos rejection of her had stung so hard, resumed familial relations. Ironically a marriage certificate was worth more in his eyes than her manifold literary achievements and honours. The couple spent an ill-fated honeymoon on the Continent, which was cut short when Cross, suffering from depression, dramatically threw himself from their balcony into the Grand Canal in Venice. Returning to London, they took up residence in Cross's house in Chelsea, but spent less than six months together. Eliot died on 22 December 1880, having just turned 61. She is buried next to Lewes in Highgate cemetery.

# Notes

## PROLOGUE: APPROACHING ELIOT

1. Bessie R. Belloc, 'Dorothea Casaubon and George Eliot', *Contemporary Review*, 65 (Feb. 1894), 213, cited in *GEB* 103.
2. Haight cites a letter to Eliot from Benjamin Jowett, the Master of Balliol College, Oxford, in which he mentions that 'friends with whom [he is] staying are very desirous of sending you a box of game' in appreciation of *Middlemarch* (*GEB* 450–1).
3. Lord Acton, 'George Eliot's Life', *Nineteenth Century*, 17 (1885), 485. Cited in Bernard Semmel, *George Eliot and the Politics of National Inheritance* (New York: Oxford University Press, 1994), 3.
4. George Eliot had multiple names. She was baptized as Mary Anne Evans, in 1837 spelled her name Mary Ann, and by 1850 had become Marian. By 1880 she had reverted to Mary Ann. Her close friends and Lewes called her Polly or Polyan, while Lewes's sons and various female friends called her Mutter or Mother. On this see Chapter 2. John Cross called her Aunt, until he called her Wife. With Lewes she called herself Mrs Lewes and later she became Mrs John Cross.
5. G. M. Young *Victorian England: Portrait of an Age* (1936; repr. Garden City, NY: Doubleday-Anchor, 1954), 15–17. Cited in Semmel, *George Eliot*, 3.
6. F. R. Leavis, *The Great Tradition* (1948; repr. Harmondsworth: Penguin, 1980).
7. Alan W. Bellringer, *George Eliot* (Basingstoke: Macmillan, 1993), 17.
8. Agnes outlived both Lewes and Eliot, dying at the age of 80 in 1902.
9. Phyllis Rose has a particularly good account of their relationship in *Parallel Lives: Five Victorian Marriages* (London: Hogarth Press, 1984), 193–238.
10. It was Herbert Spencer and John Chapman, the editor of the *Westminster Review*, for whom she had worked for a number of years, that spread the word. On this episode, see *GEB* 287–92. Eliot's romantic feelings towards her close friend Herbert Spencer were not reciprocated; and it is likely that her relationship with Chapman was more intimate than that of the professional colleagues they had been.

11. *Athenaeum*, 2 July 1859, 20. Cited in *GEB* 290.
12. J. W. Cross, *George Eliot's Life as Related in Her Letters and Journals*, 3 vols. (Edinburgh: William Blackwood, 1885), iii. 376.
13. The manuscript of Simcox's journal, 'Autobiography of a Shirt Maker' (1876–1900), is held in the Bodleian Library. It was used extensively by Haight. On Simcox and Eliot, see K. A. McKenzie, *Edith Simcox and George Eliot* (Oxford: Oxford University Press, 1961), and Norma Vince, 'The Fiddler, the Angel and the Defiance of Antigone: A Reading of Edith Simcox's "Autobiography of a Shirtmaker"', *Women: A Cultural Review*, 6/2 (1995), 143–65.
14. Lewes had, in fact, grown up in France, but had been educated in England.
15. Rosemary Ashton's highly acclaimed biography, *George Eliot: A Life* (London: Hamish Hamilton, 1996), regrettably has been published too recently for me to draw on.
16. See Suzanne Graver, *George Eliot and Community: A Study in Social Theory and Fictional Form* (Berkeley and Los Angeles: University of California Press, 1984).
17. See Gillian Beer, *George Eliot* (Brighton: Harvester Press, 1986), and Kathleen Blake, '*Middlemarch* and the Woman Question', *Nineteenth-Century Fiction*, 31 (1976), 285–312.
18. See Gillian Beer, *Darwin's Plots: Evolutionary Narratives in Darwin, George Eliot and Nineteenth-Century Fiction* (London: Routledge & Kegan Paul, 1983), George Levine, *Darwin and the Novelists: Patterns of Science in Victorian Fiction* (Cambridge, Mass.: Harvard University Press, 1988), Nancy Paxton, *George Eliot and Herbert Spencer* (Princeton, NJ: Princeton University Press, 1991), Diane Postlethwaite, *Making it Whole: A Victorian Circle and the Shape of their World* (Columbus, Oh.: Ohio State University Press, 1984), Lawrence Rothfield, *Vital Signs: Medical Realism in Nineteenth-Century Fiction* (Princeton, NJ: Princeton University Press, 1992), 84–119, Sally Shuttleworth, *George Eliot and Nineteenth-Century Science: The Make-Believe of a Beginning* (Cambridge: Cambridge University Press, 1984), Mark Wormald, 'Microscopy and Semiotic in *Middlemarch*', *Nineteenth-Century Literature*, 50/4 (1996), 501–24.

## CHAPTER 1. VAGUE DREAMS: REALISM AND THE DRAMA OF DETAILS

1. *Supererogatory* is a term meaning superfluous or excessive, usually used in theological contexts to mean good acts beyond those required by God.

2. Mrs Jellyby, the philanthropist, in Dickens's *Bleak House* (1853) is at the receiving end of a similar attack. Like Mr Brooke, she is castigated for her interest in Africa that blinds her to the degeneracy of her own family, the decline of her own home.
3. *Daniel Deronda* presents a much more cosmopolitan world view, but there is a way of reading even this as a novel that is fundamentally about the repair of the home. In this case, however, 'home' is understood specifically as the nation, England. Thus, when Daniel sets out for 'the East' at the end of the novel, to found a Jewish homeland, he provides a model for the strengthening and rejuvenation of a national culture that should be brought to bear on England. As we shall see, this novel raises a different set of political issues and attitudes to earlier works, but it nevertheless shares with them a strong belief in the importance of the idea of 'home'. On this, see Chapter 3.
4. On the social applications of organic theory, see Suzanne Graver, *George Eliot and Community: A Study in Social Theory and Fictional Form* (Berkeley and Los Angeles: University of California Press, 1984).
5. Thomas Carlyle's work provides a strong example of the ideological uses of the idea of the organic. See, for example, his essay, 'Signs of the Times' (1821).
6. On the *Bildungsroman* and the origins of the novel, see Ian Watt, *The Rise of the Novel* (London: Chatto & Windus, 1957), and Michael McKeon, *The Origins of the English Novel, 1600–1740* (Baltimore, Md.: Johns Hopkins University Press, 1987).
7. For a brilliant account of the ideological content of *Adam Bede,* see Terry Eagleton, *Criticism and Ideology: A Study in Marxist Literary Theory* (London: Verso, 1976), 110–16.
8. During the course of the novel, the workplace and the home are separated from each other. In this, the novel corresponds with the process of embourgeoisement that Leonore Davidoff and Catherine Hall analyse in their *Family Fortunes: Men and Women of the English Middle Class, 1780–1850* (London: Hutchinson, 1987).
9. In contrast to this, in the earlier scenes Lisbeth and Dolly are both clearly differentiated from the doors in which they are framed.
10. See Sandra Gilbert and Susan Gubar, *The Madwoman in the Attic: The Woman Writer and the Nineteenth-Century Literary Imagination* (New Haven, Conn.: Yale University Press, 1979), one of the first works to explore this dynamic in Eliot's work. See also Nina Auerbach, 'The Power of Hunger: Demonism and Maggie Tulliver', *Nineteenth-Century Fiction*, 30 (1975), 150–71. More recent discussions of gender in *Adam Bede* include Margaret Homans, 'Dinah's Blush, Maggie's Arm: Class, Gender and Sexuality in George Eliot's Early Novels', *Victorian Studies*, 36/2 (1993), 155–78, and Jill L.

Matus, *Unstable Bodies, Victorian Representations of Sexuality and Maternity* (Manchester: Manchester University Press, 1995), 167–78, which is particularly insightful in relation to Hetty.

11. Eliot and Lewes were ambivalent about the uses of Joseph Liggins, who now lived in the Isle of Man, and had in fact claimed to be George Eliot. Whilst his existence provided an excellent decoy for maintaining Eliot's anonymity, on the other hand, they were reluctant to see him usurp the credit for the works. See *GEB* 280–91.
12. On Eliot and Dutch and Flemish genre painting, see Hugh Witemeyer, *George Eliot and the Visual Arts* (New Haven, Conn.: Yale University Press, 1979), 105–25.
13. The idea of the mirror is explored by Erich Auerbach in his seminal study of realism in European literature, *Mimesis: Representations of Reality in Western Literature*, trans. William R. Trask (1946; repr. Princeton, NJ: Princeton University Press, 1968).
14. For a stimulating account of the relationship between legal evidence and the development of the novel, see Alexander Welsh, *Strong Representations: Narrative and Circumstantial Evidence in England* (Baltimore, Md.: Johns Hopkins University Press, 1992). Welsh's argument is, broadly, that the novel's development as a genre coincides with the increasing use of circumstantial evidence in legal cases in the late eighteenth and nineteenth centuries. See also Welsh's study of Eliot, *George Eliot and Blackmail* (Cambridge, Mass.: Harvard University Press, 1985).
15. J. Hillis Miller, 'Optics and Semiotics in *Middlemarch*', in Jerome H. Buckley (ed.), *The Worlds of Victorian Fiction* (Cambridge, Mass.: Harvard University Press, 1975), 125–45.
16. Michel Foucault, *The Birth of the Clinic*, trans. A. M. Sheridan (1973; repr. London: Routledge, 1986).
17. Ibid. 124–48.
18. On the microscope in *Middlemarch*, see Mark Wormald, 'Microscopy and Semiotic in *Middlemarch*', *Nineteenth-Century Literature*, 50/4 (1996), 501–24.
19. See Lawrence Rothfield, *Vital Signs: Medical Realism in Nineteenth-Century Fiction* (Princeton, NJ: Princeton University Press, 1992), 84–119. Rothfield situates *Middlemarch* in the context of debates in science and medicine, not in the 1820s and 1830s, the time in which the novel is set, but rather in the 1860s and 1870s, the time of writing. He points out Eliot's and Lewes's shared concern for the dehumanization of science. He also suggests that, in the late 1860s and 1870s, developments in cell theory which emphasized the independent life of cells were uneasily incorporated into clinical medicine, in which the suffering of the patient as a whole person, rather than as a collection of cells, took precedence. He argues that

'the complexity of [Eliot's] ideological role [as an organicist] demands an analysis that respects the immanent problematics of the first instance – that of the conflict of the sciences' (p. 99).

20. See, for instance, Rothfield, *Vital Signs*.

## CHAPTER 2. REGENERATION: THE USES OF THE FAMILY

1. This was on account of the renunciation of her religious beliefs. They were reconciled with one another six months later, when Eliot agreed to attend church again. Eliot continued to live with him until his death in 1849.
2. See *GEB* 452.
3. She was 'Mutter' to Lewes's sons, 'Madre' to Emilia Pattison, 'Mother' to Elma Stewart. Edith Simcox addressed her as 'Mother' by Eliot's request, but later Eliot withdrew the offer. On this, see Norma Vince, 'The Fiddler, the Angel and the Defiance of Antigone: A Reading of Edith Simcox's "Autobiography of a Shirtmaker"', *Women: A Cultural Review*, 6/2 (1995), 157–9.
4. Friends speculated that they took measures against having children. See *GEB* 205.
5. 'I have said that Poetry is the spontaneous overflow of powerful feelings: it takes its origins from emotion recollected in tranquillity: the emotion is contemplated till by a species of reaction the tranquillity gradually disappears, and an emotion, similar to that which was before the subject of contemplation, is gradually produced...'(William Wordsworth, 'Preface to the *Lyrical Ballads*' (1800), in *Prose Works* ed. W. J. B. Owen and Jane Worthington Smyser 3 vols. (Oxford: Clarendon Press, 1974), i. 148.
6. As we saw in Chapter 1, in 'How I came to write fiction' she is quite explicit about Lewes's formative role in her career as a novelist. Indeed, she writes that her first piece of fiction was conceived in bed with George: 'one morning as I was lying in bed, thinking what should be the subject of my first story, my thoughts merged themselves into a dreamy doze, and I imagined myself writing a story of which the title was – 'The Sad Fortunes of the Reverend Amos Barton'. I was soon wide awake again, and told G. He said, "O what a capital title!"' (See *L.* ii. 407; cf. Phyllis Rose, *Parallel Lives: Five Victorian Marriages* (London: Hogarth Press, 1984), 221).
7. See, e.g., Ruby Redinger, *George Eliot: The Emergent Self* (London: Bodley Head, 1976), and Dianne Sadoff, *Monsters of Affection: Dickens, Eliot and Brontë on Fatherhood* (Baltimore, Md.: Johns Hopkins University Press, 1982).
8. Literally a living picture, the tableau vivant was an art form that

enjoyed considerable popularity throughout the Victorian period, whereby actors would perform scenes represented in familiar paintings. Gwendolen and her cousins perform an ill-fated tableau vivant in *Daniel Deronda*. On the tableau vivant, see Richard D. Altick, *The Shows of London* (Cambridge, Mass.: Bellknap, Harvard University Press, 1978), 342–9.

9. Unsigned review of *Romola* in *Westminster Review*, 80 (Oct. 1863), 344–52, repr. in David Carroll (ed.), *George Eliot: The Critical Heritage* (London: Routledge & Kegan Paul, 1971), 217.
10. The extent to which Eliot subscribed to or distanced herself from positivist beliefs has been the centre of much critical debate, particularly in relation to *Romola*, the novel considered by many to be the closest to a positivist work. See Bernard Semmel, *George Eliot and the Politics of National Inheritance* (New York: Oxford University Press, 1994) 55–77, T. R. Wright, 'George Eliot and Positivism: A Reassessment', *Modern Language Review* 76/2 (1981); 257–72, and Nancy L. Paxton, 'Feminism and Positivism in George Eliot's *Romola*' in Rhoda Nathan (ed.), *Nineteenth Century Women Writers* (Westport, Conn.: Greenwood, 1986) 143–50.
11. George Henry Lewes's and Eliot's interest in embryology and the related topic of cell theory is reflected in their library of scientific books, now kept at Dr Williams's Library in London. See William Baker (ed.), *The George Eliot – George Henry Lewes Library* (New York: Garland, 1977). The Library contains C. F. Wolff's *Theorie von der Generation* (Berlin, 1764), and works by Xavier Bichat and William Lawrence. It also contains Joseph Kahn's illustrated embryological guide, *Atlas of the Formation of the Human Body* (London, 1852). Kahn's book is a work directed to a popular audience, and the edition in the Eliot–Lewes library contains marginalia by Lewes.
12. Sally Shuttleworth, *George Eliot and Nineteenth-Century Science: The Make-Believe of a Beginning* (Cambridge: Cambridge University Press, 1984), 11–12.
13. Jules Law, 'Water Rights and the "Crossing o' Breeds": Chiastic Exchange in *The Mill on the Floss*' in Linda M. Shires (ed.), *Rewriting the Victorians: Theory, History and the Politics of Gender* (London: Routledge, 1992) 52–69.
14. This was a theme that had been explored by British writers too. William Cooke Taylor's *The Natural History of Society* (1840) was one of a number of works in this period that set out to analyse society as though it were a natural organism.
15. Robert J. C. Young, *Colonial Desire: Hybridity in Theory, Culture and Race* (London: Routledge, 1995) 6–19.
16. John Sibree, brother of her friend Mary Sibree, became Eliot's correspondent in 1846. Sibree at this stage was studying for the

Independent ministry, following in his father's footsteps. Sibree's published works include his translation of Hegel's *Lectures on the Philosophy of History* (1857), *Human Anatomy Simplified in a Course of Three Elementary Lectures* (1854), and three volumes of poetry.

17. Eliot's ideas in this letter are probably derived from J. C. Prichard, *The Natural History of Man* (1843). On Prichard, see Young, *Colonial Desire*, 10–11. The terms of amalgamation are taken up interestingly in *The Mill on the Floss* in a discussion of forms of sociability between boys, here specifically, between Tom Tulliver and the 'humpback', Philip Wakem: 'If boys and men are to be welded together in the glow of transient feeling, they must be made of metal that will mix: else they inevitably fall asunder when the heat dies out' (*MF* 261–2).
18. Esther's position is similar to that of the eponymous heroine of Charlotte Brontë's *Jane Eyre* (1847). On this novel, Eliot wrote to Charles Bray: '[I] shall be glad to know what you admire in it. All self-sacrifice is good – but one would like it to be in a somewhat nobler cause than that of a diabolical law which chains a man soul and body to a putrefying carcase. However the book *is* interesting...' (*L.* i. 268).
19. Eliot expanded on this message in a piece commissioned by *Blackwood's Edinburgh Magazine* in January 1868 entitled 'Address to Working Men, by Felix Holt'.
20. Eliot began work on *The Spanish Gypsy* in 1864, but abandoned it, concentrating on her new novel, *Felix Holt*, which she began in 1865. *The Spanish Gypsy* was resumed in the summer of 1866. It was eventually published in June 1868.

## CHAPTER 3. THE SHADOW OF THE COMING AGE: MODERNITY AND THE LIMITS OF REALISM

1. This is certainly the case with 'The Lifted Veil'. Eliot herself was uneasy about the work, declaring in 1873 that she felt it 'not...judicious to reprint it at present' (*L.* v. 380). On the early reception of the work, see Beryl Gray, 'Afterword', in *The Lifted Veil* (London: Virago, 1985). The reprinting of the work in 1985 by Virago coincided with a resurgence of critical interest in the work. Sandra Gilbert and Susan Gubar focus on this minor work in their assessment of Eliot in *The Madwoman in the Attic: The Woman Writer and the Nineteenth-Century Literary Imagination* (New Haven, Conn.: Yale University Press, 1979), 443–77. See also Mary Jacobus, 'Hysterics Suffer Mainly from Reminiscences', in *Reading Women:*

*Essays in Feminist Criticism* (New York: Columbia University Press, 1986), 246–74. *The Impressions of Theophrastus Such*, on the other hand, has still been paid very little critical attention, although two recent editions have been produced, one edited by D. J. Enright (London: Everyman, 1995), and the other edited by Nancy Henry (London: Pickering & Chatto, 1994).

2. On conversion narratives, see Michael Ragussis, *Figures of Conversion: The Jewish Question and English National Identity* (Durham, NC: Duke University Press, 1995). See also Brian Cheyette, *Constructions of 'The Jew' in English Literature and Society: Racial Representations, 1875–1945* (Cambridge: Cambridge University Press, 1993), 43–53.
3. On this see Alice Shalvi (ed.), *'Daniel Deronda': A Centenary Symposium* (Jerusalem: Jerusalem Academic Press, 1976). For a specific example of the role of Eliot's work in the identity formation of the young Jewish–American poet Emma Lazarus, see Anne Janowitz, 'Torch Songs: The Poetry, Politics and Identity of Emma Lazarus', *Jewish Quarterly* (Spring, 1996), 37–41.
4. F. R. Leavis, *The Great Tradition* (1948; repr. Harmondsworth: Penguin, 1980), 97–147.
5. On the crowds in Eliot's earlier works, see Joseph Butwin, 'The Pacification of the Crowd: From "Janet's Repentance" to *Felix Holt, Nineteenth-Century Fiction*, 35/3 (1980), 349–71.
6. On the crowd, see Elias Canetti, *Crowds and Power*, trans. Carol Steward (London: Penguin, 1973).
7. Eliot emphasized throughout physiognomical features, such as Daniel's darkness, and the set of his eyes. On the physiognomy of the Jew, see Robert Knox, *The Races of Men* (1850; 2nd edn., London: Renshaw, 1862), esp. 196–7. But, as critics have noted, Daniel's racial identity would also have been inscribed on his body in circumcision. See K. M. Newton, '*Daniel Deronda* and Circumcision', in *In Defence of Literary Interpretation: Theory and Practice* (London: Macmillan Press, 1986), 197–211 (repr. in K. M. Newton (ed.), *George Eliot* (London: Longman, 1991), 218–31), and, on the interpretative implications of circumcision, Cynthia Chase, 'The Decomposition of the Elephants: Double-Reading *Daniel Deronda*', *PMLA*, 93 (1978), 215–27, and Mary Wilson Carpenter, 'The Apocalypse of the Old Testament: *Daniel Deronda* and the Interpretation of Interpretation', *PMLA*, 99 (1984), 56–71.
8. On Eliot's links with fringe science, see Diana Postlethwaite, *Making it Whole: A Victorian Circle and the Shape of their World* (Columbia, Oh.: Ohio State University Press, 1984).
9. See Adam Crabtree, *From Mesmer to Freud: Magnetic Sleep and the Roots of Psychological Healing* (New Haven, Conn.: Yale University Press, 1993).

10. See Roger Cooter, *The Cultural Meaning of Popular Science: Phrenology and the Organisation of Consent in Nineteenth-Century Britain* (Cambridge: Cambridge University Press, 1984).
11. This idea was explored thoroughly by scientists such as S. G. Morton, whose works provided a compendious record of the different peoples of the world according to the shape of their heads. See, for instance, S. G. Morton, *Crania Americana: or, a Comparative View of the Skulls of Various Aboriginal Nations of North and South America* (1839).
12. For instance, Eliot's perceived dependence on Lewes is thematized in Haight's biography.
13. Recognizing the eccentricity of the work, Eliot described it as 'a slight story of an outré kind' (*GEB* 269), but her publishers found it something of an embarrassment. William Blackwood thought it 'strange that George Eliot should have written it', and John Blackwood – who put the work down to an aberration caused by Eliot's distress at the time, at the revelation of her true identity in the London literary circles – tactfully wrote that he 'wish[ed] the theme had been a happier one' (*GEB* 296–7). Cf. note 1 above.
14. On sensation fiction, see Lyn Pykett, *The Sensation Novel: From 'The Woman in White' to 'The Moonstone'* (Plymouth: Northcote House Press, 1994).
15. Lewes's arguments are succinctly laid out in his two-part essay, 'Spiritualism and Materialism', *Fortnightly Review*, 19 (1871), 479–93, 707–19.
16. On Lewes's contribution to the developing science of psychology, see L. S. Hearnshaw, *A Short History of British Psychology, 1840–1940* (London: Methuen, 1964), 46–52.
17. Lewes, 'Spiritualism and Materialism', 492.
18. Jacqueline Rose, 'George Eliot and the Spectacle of the Woman', in *Sexuality and the Field of Vision* (London: Verso, 1986), 105–22.
19. See, e.g. Charles Elam, *Winds of a Doctrine, Being an Examination of the Modern Theory of Automatism and Evolution* (London, 1876), and W. B. Carpenter, *Is Man an Automaton: A Lecture* (1886). Lewes devotes a long section to the problem of automatism in *Problems of Life and Mind*. He comes to the conclusion, however, that 'The question of automatism ... may, I think be summarily disposed of by a reference to the irresistible evidence each man carries in his own consciousness that his actions are frequently – even if not always – determined by feeling ... I am not a machine .... (*The Physical Basis of Mind*, in *Problems of Life and Mind*, 2nd ser. (London: Trübner, 1877), 409.
20. *The Physical Basis of Mind*, 375.
21. *Athenaeum*, 7 June 1879. Cited by Enright, *TS*, p. xxvii.

# Select Bibliography

## WORKS BY GEORGE ELIOT

Where relevant, dates given are those of the first edition of the works in book form. The Cabinet Edition of the works, corrected by the author, was published by William Blackwood in 1878–80.


### Fiction

*Scenes of Clerical Life* (Edinburgh and London: William Blackwood, 1858).

*Adam Bede* (Edinburgh and London: William Blackwood, 1859).

'The Lifted Veil', *Blackwood's Edinburgh Magazine* (July, 1859).

*The Mill on the Floss* (Edinburgh and London: William Blackwood, 1860).

*Silas Marner: The Weaver of Raveloe* (Edinburgh and London: William Blackwood, 1861).

*Romola* (London: Smith, Elder and Co., 1963).

'Brother Jacob', *Cornhill Magazine* (July, 1864).

*Felix Holt: The Radical* (Edinburgh and London: William Blackwood, 1866).

*Middlemarch: A Study of Provincial Life* (Edinburgh and London: William Blackwood, 1871).

*Daniel Deronda* (Edinburgh and London: William Blackwood, 1876).

### Poetry

*The Spanish Gypsy: A Poem* (Edinburgh and London: William Blackwood, 1868).

*The Legend of Jubal and other Poems* (Edinburgh and London: William Blackwood, 1874).

### Other Works

Strauss, David Friedrich, *The Life of Jesus Critically Examined*, trans. from the 4th German ed. by Marian Evans (London (no publ.), 1846).

Feuerbach, Ludwig, *The Essence of Christianity*, trans., from the 2nd edn.

by Marian Evans (London: John Chapman, 1854).
Spinoza, *Ethics*, trans. George Eliot (Salzburg: Universität Salzburg, 1981).
*The Impressions of Theophrastus Such* (Edinburgh: William Blackwood, 1879).
*The George Eliot Letters*, ed. Gordon S. Haight, 9 vols. (New Haven, Conn.: Yale University Press, 1954–5, 1978).
*Essays of George Eliot*, ed. Thomas Pinney (London: Routledge & Kegan Paul, 1963).
*George Eliot: Writer's Notebook, 1854–79*, ed. Joseph Wiesenfarth (Virginia: University of Virginia Press, 1985).

## BIOGRAPHY

There are many biographies of Eliot. The best are as follows.

Ashton, Rosemary, *George Eliot: A Life* (London: Hamish Hamilton, 1996).
Cross, J. W. *George Eliot's Life as Related in her Letters and Journals*, (3 vols. Edinburgh and London: William Blackwood, 1885).
Haight, G. S., *George Eliot: A Biography* (Oxford: Clarendon Press, 1968). For many years, this has been the standard life of Eliot.
Redinger, Ruby, *George Eliot: The Emergent Self* (London: Bodley Head; Toronto: Random House, 1975). Psychobiography which emphasizes Eliot's family relationships and the formative impact of her early childhood.

## CRITICAL WORKS

The critical literature on Eliot is enormous and very rich. For a more extensive annotated bibliography, see J. McDonagh, 'George Eliot' in *Annotated Bibliography for English Studies* (Lisse, NL: Swets and Zeilinger, 1997) vol. 3.

Armstrong, Isobel, *Victorian Poetry: Poetry, Poetics and Politics* (London: Routledge, 1993), 370–2. Very suggestive discussion of Eliot's poetry, particularly *The Spanish Gypsy*.
Ashton, Rosemary, *George Eliot* (Oxford: Oxford University Press, 1983).
Auerbach, Nina, 'The Power of Hunger: Demonism and Maggie Tulliver', *Nineteenth-Century Fiction*, 30 (1975), 150–71. Influential reading of *The Mill on the Floss* as a gothic romance. In so far as the novel is autobiographical, Auerbach argues, Maggie is an expression not of a woman with a 'masculine intellect', as is frequently

suggested, but rather of the conventionally feminine.

Beatty, James, *'Middlemarch': From Notebook to Novel: A Study of George Eliot's Creative Method* (Berkeley and Los Angeles: University of California Press, 1960).

Beer, Gillian, *Darwin's Plots: Evolutionary Narratives in Darwin, George Eliot and Nineteenth-Century Fiction* (London: Routledge & Kegan Paul, 1983). A ground-breaking study of the impact of Darwin's theory of evolution on narrative fiction in the period.

——— *George Eliot* (Brighton: Harvester Press, 1986). One of the most challenging and rewarding of the introductory works on Eliot. Beer focuses on Eliot's responses to contemporary debates about women and situates her works alongside those of other women writers of the period.

Blake, Kathleen, '*Middlemarch* and the Woman Question', *Nineteenth-Century Fiction*, 31 (1976), 285–312.

Bodenheimer, Rosemarie, *The Real Life of Mary Ann Evans: George Eliot, Her Letters and Fiction* (Ithaca, NY: Cornell University Press, 1994).

Bonaparte, Felicia, *The Triptych and the Cross: The Central Myths of George Eliot's Poetic Imagination* (Brighton: Harvester, 1979).

Brantlinger, Patrick, 'Nations and Novels: Disraeli, George Eliot and Orientalism', *Victorian Studies*, 35 (1992), 255–75.

Butwin, Joseph, 'The Pacification of the Crowd: From "Janet's Repentance" to *Felix Holt*', *Nineteenth-Century Fiction*, 35/3 (1980), 349–71.

Carpenter, Mary Wilson, 'The Apocalypse of the Old Testament: *Daniel Deronda* and the Interpretation of Interpretation', *PMLA*, 99 (1984), 56–71.

Carroll, David (ed.), *George Eliot: The Critical Heritage* (London: Routledge & Kegan Paul, 1971). An anthology of critical responses to the works, from the early reviews to assessments in the 1960s.

Chase, Cynthia, 'The Decomposition of the Elephants: Double-Reading *Daniel Deronda*', *PMLA*, 93/2 (1978), 216–27. A deconstructive reading of *Daniel Deronda*. Chase addresses the double structure of the novel, not in terms of the two plots, but in terms of two interpretative strategies: that of the omniscient narrator of realism, and that of the deconstructive narrative, characterized by Merrick's letter to Deronda. The latter enables us to see that the novel – and realist narrative more broadly – consistently reverses cause and effect, so that, for instance, Daniel's revealed Jewishness is seen as an effect of his interest in Judaism, rather than vice versa.

Cheyette, Brian, *Constructions of 'The Jew' in English Literature and Society: Racial Representations, 1875–1945* (Cambridge: Cambridge University Press, 1993), 45–53. Helpful discussion of *Daniel Deronda* and the political, cultural, and social issues relating to Jews.

Cunningham, Valentine, *Everywhere Spoken Against: Dissent in the Victorian Novel* (Oxford: Clarendon Press, 1975). A study of evangelism and dissent in the Victorian novel – a central issue in Eliot's work. The chapter on Eliot focuses on Dinah Morris and Rufus Lyon, and explains the theological, political, and social implications of dissent.

Doody, Mary Ann, 'George Eliot and the Eighteenth-Century Novel', *Nineteenth-Century Fiction*, 35 (1980), 260–91.

Eagleton, Terry, *Criticism and Ideology: A Study in Marxist Literary Theory*, (London: Verso, 1976).

——— 'Power and Knowledge in "The Lifted Veil"', *Literature and History*, 9/1 (1983), 52–61. Marxist reading of 'The Lifted Veil' as an exemplification of the impossibility of escaping bourgeois ideology.

Ermarth, Elizabeth Deeds, *George Eliot* (Boston, Mass.: Twayne, 1985). Helpful introduction to Eliot laying emphasis on her early philosophical interests. Useful material on the translations.

Gallagher, Catherine, 'George Eliot and *Daniel Deronda*: The Prostitute and the Jewish Question', in Ruth Bernard Yeazell (ed.), *Sex, Politics and Science in the Nineteenth-Century Novel* (Baltimore: Johns Hopkins University Press, 1986) 39–62. A brilliant analysis of the connections between art, economic exchange, sexuality, and Judaism in Eliot's late works, *Theophrastus Such* and *Daniel Deronda*.

——— *The Industrial Reformation of English Fiction: Social Discourse and Narrative Form, 1832–1867* (Chicago, Ill.: University of Chicago Press, 1985). An important study of the politics of representation in the industrial novel. It includes discussion of *Felix Holt* in the context of Reform.

Gilbert, Sandra, and Gubar, Susan, *The Madwoman in the Attic: The Woman Writer and the Nineteenth-Century Literary Imagination* (New Haven, Conn.: Yale University Press, 1979).

Graver, Suzanne, *George Eliot and Community: A Study in Social Theory and Fictional Form* (Berkeley and Los Angeles: University of California Press, 1984). A useful study of Eliot's idea of community in the context of contemporary social thought. Particular emphasis is given to the work of Auguste Comte, Herbert Spencer, and J. S. Mill.

Gray, Beryl, *George Eliot and Music* (London: Macmillan, 1989). An analysis of musical imagery in *Mill on the Floss, Middlemarch*, and *Daniel Deronda*.

Hardy, Barbara, *The Novels of George Eliot: A Study in Form* (London: Athlone Press, 1959). Influential work which shaped Eliot criticism for a number of decades, shifting critical attention away from moral questions towards the complexity of form in the works.

Homans, Margaret, 'Dinah's Blush, Maggie's Arm: Class, Gender and Sexuality in George Eliot's Early Novels', *Victorian Studies*, 36/2,

(1993), 155-78. A useful essay on the interactions of class and gender in *Adam Bede* and *The Mill on the Floss.*

Jacobus, Mary, 'Hysterics Suffer Mainly from Reminiscences', in *Reading Women: Essays in Feminist Criticism* (New York: Columbia University Press; London: Methuen, 1986), 246–74. Psychoanalytic reading of 'The Lifted Veil'.

——— 'The Question of Language: Men of Maxims and *The Mill on the Floss*', *Critical Inquiry*, 8/2 (1981), 206–22. A feminist reading of *The Mill on the Floss.* The character of Maggie, and the text more generally, provide examples of women's troubled relationship to language – resolved in the novel's ending, 'an imaginative reaching beyond analytic and realistic modes to the metaphors of unbounded female desire'.

Law, Jules, 'Water Rights and the "Crossing o' Breeds": Chiastic Exchange in *The Mill on the Floss*', in Linda M. Shires (ed.), *Rewriting the Victorians: Theory, History and the Politics of Gender* (London: Routledge, 1992), 52–69. New historicist reading on the river in *The Mill on the Floss.*

Levine, George, 'George Eliot's Hypothesis of Reality', *Nineteenth-Century Fiction*, 25 (1980), 1–28. A penetrating study of realism in *Middlemarch* and *Daniel Deronda*, demonstrating the scientific basis of Eliot's representation of reality drawing on intellectual relations with Lewes's *Problems of Life and Mind.*

McCann, J. Clinton Jr, 'Disease and Cure in "Janet's Repentance": George Eliot's Change of Mind', *Literature and Medicine*, 9 (1990), 69–78. A useful discussion of medical and religious references and metaphors in 'Janet's Repentance'.

Mann, Karen B., 'George Eliot and Wordsworth: The Power of Sound and the Power of the Mind', *Studies in English Literature, 1500–1900*, 20 (1980), 675–94. Exploration of the influence of Wordsworth on Eliot, particularly as evidenced in her poem 'The Legend of Jubal'.

Matus, Jill L., *Unstable Bodies: Victorian Representations of Sexuality and Maternity* (Manchester: Manchester University Press, 1995). This is a useful study of the ways in which bio-medical constructions of femininity infiltrate other cultural forms in the Victorian period. Good readings of *Adam Bede* and *Middlemarch.*

Miller, D. A., *Narrative and Its Discontents: Problems of Closure in the Traditional Novel* (Princeton, NJ.: Princeton University Press, 1981), esp. 'The Wisdom of Balancing Claims', pp. 107–94. A brilliant and important discussion of the narrative strategies in *Middlemarch*, showing that it is both an exemplary realist text, but also a worrying and disruptive text.

Miller, J. Hillis, 'Narrative and History', *English Literary History*, 41, (1974), 455–73. A deconstructive approach to *Middlemarch.* Miller argues that, although the novel is usually taken to be an example of a realist text that confirms 'metaphysical' notions of history – a belief in progress, and an homogeneous idea of time – this reading fails to notice that the novel in fact critiques this idea, and proposes instead an idea of history 'consonant with those of Nietzsche and Benjamin'. In this sense, 'history is an act of repetition in which the present takes possession of the past, and liberates it for a present purpose…'.

——— 'Optics and Semiotics in *Middlemarch*', in Jerome H. Buckley (ed.), *The Worlds of Victorian Fiction* (Cambridge Mass.: Harvard University Press, 1975), 125–45. An analysis of Eliot's realism that shows how it is constructed through the use of different and conflicting metaphorical systems for totalizing vision.

Miller, Nancy, 'Emphasis Added: Plots and Plausibilities in Women's Fiction', *PMLA*, 96/1 (1981), 36–48. Another feminist reading of *The Mill on the Floss*, which focuses on the plots rather than language. *The Mill on the Floss* is a woman's text that protests against the 'reality' that is established by the patriarchal division of labour that destines women only for romantic love.

Newton, K. M. (ed.), *George Eliot* (London: Longman, 1991). A very good anthology of recent essays on Eliot, adopting a range of different theoretical approaches.

Noble, Thomas A., *George Eliot's 'Scenes of Clerical Life'*, (New Haven, Conn.: Yale University Press, 1965). Still the only extended study of *Scenes of Clerical Life*.

Nunokawa, Jeff, 'The Miser's Two Bodies: *Silas Marner* and the Sexual Possibility of the Commodity', *Victorian Studies*, 36/3 (1993), 273–92. Brilliant study of alienated labour and alienated sexuality in *Silas Marner*.

Paxton, Nancy L., 'Feminism and Positivism in George Eliot's *Romola*', in Rhoda Nathan (ed.), *Nineteenth-Century Women Writers* (Westport, Conn.: Greenwood, 1986), 143–50.

——— *George Eliot and Herbert Spencer: Feminism, Evolution and the Reconstruction of Gender*, (Princeton, NJ: Princeton University Press, 1991).

Peck, John (ed.), *Middlemarch* (Basingstoke: Macmillan, 1992). In the New Casebook series, a collection of critical works on *Middlemarch*.

Postlethwaite, Diana, *Making it Whole: A Victorian Circle and the Shape of their World* (Columbia, Oh.: Ohio State University Press, 1984). Discussion of Eliot and the coterie of fringe scientists of which she was a part.

Ragussis, Michael, *Figures of Conversion: The Jewish Question and English National Identity* (Durham, NC: Duke University Press, 1995). Excellent discussion of *The Spanish Gypsy* and *Daniel Deronda* in terms of religious conversion narratives.

Reilly, Jim, *Shadowtime: History and Representation in Hardy, Conrad, and George Eliot* (London: Routledge, 1993). A challenging study of Eliot's works in the context of nineteenth- and twentieth-century debates about history and historical representation. Reilly argues that Eliot's works present glimpses of an anti-realist project, suggesting an alliance with Marx rather than Hegel, which he traces through the Frankfurt School to post-structuralist writers. Includes readings of *Silas Marner*, *Romola*, and *Daniel Deronda*.

Rodstein, Susan de Sola, 'Sweetness and Dark: George Eliot's "Brother Jacob"', *Modern Language Quarterly*, 52 (1991), 295–317. There are very few treatments of this minor work, but this essay makes a good case for drawing it into the critical frame. Rodstein takes a historicist approach, analysing references to the sugar trade in the context of the history of slavery and imperialism.

Rose, Jacqueline, 'George Eliot and the Spectacle of the Woman', in *Sexuality and the Field of Vision* (London: Verso, 1986), 105–22. Influential essay on *Daniel Deronda* and psychoanalysis, analysing Gwendolen's hysteria.

Rothfield, Lawrence, *Vital Signs: Medical Realism in Nineteenth-Century Realism* (Princeton, NJ.: Princeton University Press, 1992). Illuminating discussion of medical metaphors in *Middlemarch*.

Sadoff, Dianne F., *Monsters of Affection: Dickens, Eliot and Brontë on Fatherhood* (Baltimore, Ind.: Johns Hopkins University Press, 1982). Psychoanalytic approach to Eliot that draws on the work of Jean Laplanche and J. B. Pontalis on the origins of sexuality to explore the works in terms of Eliot's ambivalent relationship with her father.

Semmel, Bernard, *George Eliot and the Politics of National Inheritance* (New York: Oxford University Press, 1994). An informative study of the theme of inheritance in Eliot's works, demonstrating that she is an 'articulate exponent of the social-conservative politics of tradition'. Useful material on Eliot's intellectual history, including exposition of her position on Comte and the Positivists.

Shalvi, Alice (ed.), *'Daniel Deronda': A Centenary Symposium* (Jerusalem: Jerusalem Academic Press, 1976).

Shuttleworth, Sally, *George Eliot and Nineteenth-Century Science: The Make-Believe of a Beginning* (Cambridge: Cambridge University Press, 1984). An authoritative account of the impact of Eliot's immersion in social and scientific theories of organicism on her works.

Uglow, Jenny, *George Eliot* (London: Virago, 1987). A short biography followed by powerful readings of the novels. This is one of the best of the many introductory works on Eliot.

Welsh, Alexander, *George Eliot and Blackmail* (Cambridge, Mass.: Harvard University Press, 1985). A study of Eliot's work in the context of the vast increase in print culture and new forms of law enforcement that characterize the mid-nineteenth century. According to Welsh, blackmail is a preoccupation of fiction – not only for Eliot but for other writers too. A wide-ranging and provocative work.

Wiesenfarth, Joseph, *George Eliot's Mythmaking* (Heidelberg: Carl Winter, 1977).

Witemeyer, Hugh, *George Eliot and the Visual Arts* (New Haven, Conn.: Yale University Press, 1979). An account of Eliot's extensive knowledge of the visual arts, the role of painting in her theory of the novel, and the uses of painting in the novels.

Wormald, Mark, 'Microscopy and Semiotic in *Middlemarch*', *Nineteenth-Century Literature*, 50/4 (1996), 501–24.

Wright, T. R., 'George Eliot and Positivism: A Reassessment', *Modern Language Review*, 76/2 (1981), 257–72.

Zimmerman, Bonnie, 'Gwendolen Harleth and "The Girl of the Period"', in Anne Smith (ed.), *George Eliot: Centenary Essays and an Unpublished Fragment* (London: Vision Press, 1980), 196–217.

# Index